THE LAND BETWEEN

THE LAND BETWEEN

Finding God in Difficult Transitions

JEFF MANION

ZONDERVAN®

ZONDERVAN.com/
AUTHORTRACKER
follow your favorite authors

We want to hear from you. Please send your comments about this book to us in care of zreview@zondervan.com. Thank you.

ZONDERVAN

The Land Between
Copyright © 2010 by Jeff Manion

This title is also available as a Zondervan ebook.
Visit www.zondervan.com/ebooks.

This title is also available in a Zondervan audio edition.
Visit www.zondervan.fm.

Requests for information should be addressed to:

Zondervan, *Grand Rapids, Michigan 49530*

Library of Congress Cataloging-in-Publication Data

Manion, Jeff, 1962–
    The land between : finding God in difficult transitions / Jeff Manion.
        p.   cm.
    ISBN 978-0-310-32998-5 (hardcover, jacketed)
    1. Change (Psychology) — Religious aspects — Christianity. I. Title.
BV4599.5.C44M36   2010
    248.8'6 — dc22   2001019763

Cover design: Michelle Lenger
Interior design: Michelle Espinoza

Printed in the United States of America

10 11 12 13 14 15 /DCI/ 22 21 20 19 18 17 16 15 14 13 12 11 10 9 8 7 6 5 4

Affectionately dedicated to my wife, Chris.
We have now shared the journey for thirty years.

CONTENTS

Part 4: Discipline

Part 5: Growth

MY PRAYER FOR YOU

MY PRAYER FOR YOU AS YOU read this book is that God will visit you with grace in your season of transition. I pray that the barren landscape of trial will become the fertile soil for new growth. May our gracious God revive your spirit and restore your laughter. May you find him in your pain and trust him in your waiting. May the One who redeems all things meet you powerfully as you journey through the Land Between.

WELCOME TO
THE LAND BETWEEN

ONE LATE NOVEMBER MORNING WHEN I was in seventh grade, tragedy reshaped our family and segmented time — life before the accident and life after.

During the life before the accident, my parents had served together planting churches in southeastern Idaho for fifteen years. My sister, the eldest, was thirteen. My younger brothers were nine, four, and an infant. I was twelve. My dad's father had died, and my parents were hurriedly preparing to depart for the funeral in Michigan. They would need to drive through the night to make it in time. Of the five children, four of us would be sent to stay with various friends, remaining in Idaho. Jamie, my two-month-old brother, would be traveling with my parents because Mom was nursing. They planned to be gone for two weeks.

While sifting through a large box of family pictures last month, I discovered a handwritten note neatly penned by my mother thirty-five years ago. The information in the note provides instructions for the care of my nine-year-old brother, Jon, during my parents' trip. As I read the note, I was struck by Mom's neat penmanship and attention to detail in the enumerated list:

1. Hot lunch ticket to be paid on Monday — $2.25 a week.
2. Trash pickup is Thursday.
3. Jon's bedtime is 9:00.
4. Jon's bus comes at 8:35 in the morning and brings him home around 3:45.
5. Clean sheets are in the trunk. There are some in the family room too.
6. The timer on my dryer works opposite of what it should. If you have a large load, set it for about 10 minutes; if just a small load, set it for 50 – 60.
7. Our doctor in Poky [Pocatello, Idaho] is Dr. Brydon, but we also go to Dr. Thurson here in Blackfoot. It would probably be easier for you to take him to Dr. T. if he needs a doctor.

Thanks so much for helping out this way. We'll probably call a couple times to see how things are going. We're supposed to get home Dec. 15. That's a long time to be gone!

That night, on Interstate 80 in western Nebraska, our family van veered off the road and rolled several times as it crossed the median before coming to rest. My father and baby brother sustained minor injuries. Mom was thrown from the van and died hours later at the hospital in a nearby town.

We were not ready to lose her. I was not ready to lose her.

The terms *dizzying* or *disorienting* do not carry the weight of our experience as I try to adequately depict the emotional swirl of those days. The heart had been removed from our house.

Mom had always been at home when I ran down the street from the bus stop after school and flew through the front door. Our yellow house on Jewell Street was a split-level home where the landing opened to stairways leading both up and down. My daily entrance ritual began with yelling an announcement from the landing that I was home. I think I did this to discern whether Mom was upstairs or down. After the accident, I found myself mindlessly reenacting this routine from years of habit. Up the driveway, through the door, "Mom! I'm home!" And then the deafening silence slapped me with the reality that she was gone.

A few months after the accident, my father accepted a position as a teacher and administrator of a small Bible college, and our family moved to East Grand Rapids, Michigan. It is an affluent community with old brick homes, manicured lawns, and mature trees. Dad found a great buy on a nice house not far from his work, so we landed there. Socially, I did not belong.

Junior high can be awful in any town, and I could have been awkward almost anywhere. This just happens to be the setting where my awkwardness was overexposed due to my cultural illiteracy. Blackfoot, Idaho, where I had spent my grade school years, had simply not prepared me for status-conscious East Grand Rapids.

From a fashion standpoint, the footwear of choice was a specific brand of deck shoe, which I had never even seen before entrance into East Grand Rapids Middle School, gracefully perched beside Reeds Lake. Until designer jeans became the rage, straight-leg Levis were the preference. I was the kid from Idaho, wearing Wrangler jeans that were too short, Keds sneakers, and the same shirt to school every day.

Soon after our arrival to Michigan, Dad became engaged and married a young secretary and recent graduate of the Bible college where he served. Carolyn was twenty-one when she became mother to two preschoolers, a grade-schooler, and two teenagers. Carolyn has one of the most gracious spirits I have ever encountered. She is cheerful and caring, and she was a godsend to our family. Little imagination is required, however, to guess that the transition from single secretary to wife and mother of five was a bit rough.

I spent eighth grade trying to regain my balance. By the end of ninth grade, I was beginning to figure things out a bit. I changed shirts with greater regularity, I no longer wore Wranglers, and I had a few friends. I was hopeful that things might work out after all. Then, at the end of ninth grade, Dad informed us that we would be moving to Sacramento, California. I was livid. I couldn't believe I had to start the whole process all over again.

The sequence of transitions was jarring. I had begun seventh grade securely nestled in a small western town where I had spent all my grade school years. Three years, one funeral, one wedding, and two cross-country moves later, I was beginning my sophomore year in Sacramento.

I have often reflected on this season of profound disorientation and chaos. I have also reflected on God's movement and mercy during this difficult time of upheaval and transition. I suspect that this season we endured as a family enlarged my heart for others passing through similar periods of difficult transition. I was in the Land Between.

The Land Between

Tom sits in the silence of his unlit living room. It is after midnight and the kids are asleep. Today was the scheduled closing on a house, and today the closing was canceled. Not postponed, canceled. The deal fell apart. He sits in the darkness repeating the number that robs him of sleep. *Three houses*, he thinks to himself. *I've sold three houses this year. Two years ago I closed on twenty-seven homes, a house every two weeks. How much longer can I do this? How much longer can we continue to drain our retirement account to pay monthly bills? Should I find a second job until things turn around? What if things don't turn around for years? I feel like I'm bleeding cash, pillaging our future to survive the present. And if I get out of real estate sales, what else am I good at? What else could I possibly choose as a new career?*

"Three houses," he whispers aloud.

This is the Land Between—where life is not as it once was, where the future is in question.

.....

Karen fumbles for the phone in a sleepy haze. The red numerals on the alarm clock read 3:17. In the moment before "Hello," she takes a quick mental inventory: *Are all the kids home?* She is conscious enough to reason that either someone has dialed a wrong number or the family is about to receive some awful news. "Hello," she mumbles. The room spins as she hears the voice of her sister on the other end: "Karen, there's been an accident."

Tonight Karen will be hurled from her normal routine of work, church, and tennis into the land of all-night hospital vigils, an intensive care unit, and lengthy rehabilitation.

This is the Land Between—where everything normal is interrupted.

.....

For many of us, the journey into the Land Between comes suddenly, like Karen's experience or my own, with a conversation that drops into our lives like an exploding bomb.

"Your position has been eliminated."

"I don't love you anymore."

"The tumor is malignant."

"The church elders are meeting to take a vote of confidence."

"Mom, Dad, I'm pregnant."

"I'm having second thoughts about the wedding."

"Dad, uh . . . I'm at the police station."

"Your mother and I are getting a divorce."

"We're moving."

"We think Mom's had a stroke. How soon can you get to the hospital?"

In a sentence we are ripped from normality and find ourselves in a new world, as if thrown from a moving train. We tumble into the world of the unemployed. We are hurled into the land of the suddenly single, the valley of the grieving, the new vocabulary of chemotherapy, or the weekly routine of nursing home visits. In our more confident, faith-filled moments, we know that we will regain our footing and find some kind of balance in a new normal, but for now we are simply and suddenly "between" and at a loss as to how to navigate the terrain.

While some enter the land shockingly, others experience a gradual, almost imperceptible entry, like Tom the real estate agent. A marriage suffers slow but constant erosion over the years before somebody walks out. The heart of a teenager drifts slowly away from her parents and from God. Key employees are released and assets are sold off as sales figures dip steadily quarter after quarter until the company is only a shadow of what it had been eight years earlier. A parent experiences gradual memory loss, and with it her independence fades little by little. Many of us entered the Land Between not with a sudden cataclysmic conversation but with the slow march of time. And yet regardless of how we enter this space, whether jarringly or gradually, the landscape is much the same.

Ada Bible Church

For more than twenty-five years, I have had the privilege of pastoring the people of Ada Bible Church in suburban Grand Rapids, Michigan. My core gifting and joy is that of digging deeply into the story of the Bible and then presenting this story, the journey of God and his people, in a way that I hope encourages life transformation. As I stand and open the Scriptures each weekend, I am often conscious of the array of chaos represented in the room. Weekly, I have the unspeakable privilege of bringing the story of God to the recently unemployed and to the terminally ill, to parents whose sons are in prison and to those who long to be parents but remain childless. Unbelievably, my calling is to speak God's mercy into the lives of those whose engagements have just fallen through or whose homes refuse to sell, to offer hope to those who may have just lowered the casket of a husband, wife, brother, sister, or child into the soil.

I firmly believe that the Land Between—that space where we feel lost or lonely or deeply hurt—is fertile ground for our spiritual transformation and for God's grace to be revealed in magnificent ways. But in addition to being the bearer of mercy, I also have the privilege of challenging God's people to holiness, and while the Land Between is prime real estate for faith transformation, it is also the space where we can grow resentful, bitter, and caustic if our responses are unguarded. The wilderness where faith can thrive is the very desert where it can dry up and die if we are not watchful.

The narrative in the Bible where we most clearly see this dynamic played out is in the desert wanderings of the Israelites. The season in the wilderness occurs after the sons and daughters of Jacob have been released from slavery in Egypt and before they reach the Promised Land. The story is near the beginning of the Bible and chronicles some of the first fumbling steps of the Israelites as a people. As we drop in to observe their distressing reaction to their desert conditions, we will glean insight into the unique challenges, temptations, and opportunities of the Land Between. As we move through the desert story together, I will pull in additional portions of Scripture that can provide added guidance as we make our way through these undesired transitions.

The drama that unfolds before us includes a leader at the

point of emotional collapse, a rancorous people spewing disheartened complaint, God's gracious provision for the one, and his swift, harsh discipline — which is also his mercy — for the other. As we dive into the story, we will find ourselves encouraged and warned, comforted at some points and rebuked at others. It is my sincere hope that we emerge from the narrative desiring to be people of deeper faith. A faith worth having.

This book is not intended to be a how-to manual on locating a swift exit ramp from the Land Between. I will not give counsel on career selection, job hunting, or debt management. I offer no advice on changing the heart of your rebellious teenager or the behavior patterns of your husband or wife. Instead, consider me your tour guide who will describe the terrain of the Land Between so we can travel through it with greater skill and grace, arriving on the other side with a deeper, richer faith. My desire is to portray the challenges and opportunities that are unique to life in the desert. For instance, we will have to wrestle with some critical questions along the way: Is it possible to possess a vital faith that prompts you to be at your best when things are at their worst? Is it possible for the best version of you to emerge while you are passing through a season of profound disappointment, unnerving chaos, or debilitating pain?

The Land Between can be profoundly disorienting. It also provides the space for God to do some of his deepest work in our lives. Many seasoned spiritual advisers propose that this is the only space in which radical, transformational growth occurs. God intends for us to emerge from this land radically reshaped. But the process of transformational growth will not occur automatically. Our response to God while in the Land Between is what will determine whether our journey through this desert will result in deep, positive growth or spiritual decline.

People often quote a common proverb in time of pain and tragedy: "Time heals all wounds." I do not find this statement to be necessarily true. Some people heal over time, while others become deeply embittered and acidic. The Land Between usually forces us to choose one way or the other. The conditions can prove so harsh that there seems little room for neutrality. While offering us a greenhouse for growth, the Land Between can also be a desert where our faith goes to die — if we let it. The habits of the heart that we foster in this space — our responses and reactions — will determine whether the Land Between results in spiritual life or spiritual death. We choose.

PART 1

COMPLAINT

CHAPTER 1

SICK OF THIS

A SHEPHERD NAMED MOSES IS TENDING his sheep when he turns aside to see a bush that is ablaze yet not consumed with fire. Moses is an old man now. A Jew raised in the house of Pharaoh, Moses had fled to the backside of the desert after murdering an Egyptian who was oppressing one of his people. That was forty years ago. Since then he has been tending the flocks of his father-in-law in this desert. He knows the terrain, perhaps better than he wishes. But here he is faced with the most unusual sight—a bush burning but not consumed. He turns to look then covers his face as he hears God saying in effect, "I am Abraham's God. I am Isaac's God. I am Jacob's God. I chose them and called them and provided for them. Now I have chosen, called, and will provide for you" (see Exodus 3).

God reveals his plans to Moses and recruits him to deliver the children of promise from the land where for generations they have been enslaved. God says, "I have come down to rescue them from the hand of the Egyptians and to bring them up out of that land into a good and spacious land, a land flowing with milk and honey" (Exodus 3:8).

After generations of slavery in Egypt, the sons and daughters of Abraham will make their way toward Canaan, the land promised to their ancestors. They will be led out of Egypt by Moses, who reluctantly accepts his leadership charge, and God has said, "I will bring them out of Egypt and into a good and spacious land." But while "out of" the land of slavery and "into" the Land of Promise sounds like a short trip, nothing is mentioned about the amount of time the people will spend in the desert, the wilderness — the Land Between.

A Necessary Middle Space

A barren wilderness separates Egypt from Canaan, and here the Israelites will spend considerable time before moving to their new home. The desert is where they will receive the Ten Commandments — the core of their covenant with God. It is also where a portable worship tent, the tabernacle, will be built. The desert is not intended to be their final destination but rather a necessary middle space where they will be formed as a people and established in their connection to God.

But a desert, of course, is a hard place. Though Egypt was the land of slavery, suffering, and agony, it was also brimming with lush vegetation. The rich waters of the Nile caused Egypt to flourish agriculturally. Canaan, too, the people's future home, was notable for its prosperity; it was, as God described it, "the land flowing with milk and honey." But as the Israelites move from the lush, fertile home of their past to the lush, fertile home of their future, they pass through the wilderness. They are stuck in the middle, the desert, the undesired space between more desirable spaces. This middle space, the Land Between, will serve as a metaphor for the undesired transitions we, too, experience in life.

For the Israelites, their experience in the wasteland was not meant to be a waste. The Land Between was to be pivotal in their formation as a people — it was where they were to be transformed from the people of slavery into the people of God. And they needed transformation. Let us consider that as they exit Egypt, the Israelites are more fully acclimated to the world of Egyptian idolatry than they are formed by the character and presence of the God of Abraham. As we watch them exit Egypt and enter the desert, we should not imagine a neatly ordered multitude of mature followers. The Israelites are an unruly mob of recently released slaves who are prone to complaining, frequently resentful of Moses' leadership, and longing to return to Egypt with every conceivable hardship. The Israelites desperately need the spiritual formation of the desert to become the people of God. In their current condition, they do not yet know their God and are unprepared to enter the Land of Promise. The desert experience is intended to shape, mold, and refine them into a community of trust. Unfortunately, it will not be their finest hour.

For us the question remains as to whether the Land Between will be ours.

Sick and Tired of Manna

Through the events of the exodus and the wilderness journey, God intends to manifest himself, to reveal his presence and his character. He demonstrates his great power through the plagues leveled against Egypt that lead to the exodus — the exit from slavery. He miraculously provides water in the desert, and he demonstrates his care by providing a daily food substance called "manna." It's as if he is saying, "I will be your God, and you will be my people. Watch me, know me, and learn to trust me."

The Israelites, to understate the case, struggled with trusting God, and in time the provision of manna was perceived as a loathsome curse. The people became sick of eating manna month after monotonous month. What exactly was this stuff? The Hebrew word *manna* actually means "What is it?" because that was the question the Israelites asked when manna appeared on the ground with the morning dew. According to Numbers 11, "manna was like coriander seed and looked like resin. The people went around gathering it, and then ground it in a hand mill or crushed it in a mortar. They cooked it in a pot or made it into cakes. And it tasted like something made with olive oil. When the dew settled on the camp at night, the manna also came down" (vv. 7 – 9).

The Israelites would collect these flakes in the morning, grind them up or crush them with a mortar and pestle, and then boil the mushy stuff in a pot. What comes to my mind is an oatmeal-like mush type of dish. This may be wildly inaccurate, but it is the image that has lodged in my brain since childhood. Manna cakes sound better to me from a texture standpoint, but I wouldn't want to eat them meal after tedious meal. A description in Exodus 16:31 compares the taste to that of wafers made with honey, which sounds appetizing. What seemed to be the issue over time, though, was not so much the taste as the frequency with which the people had to eat manna. The Israelites had been in the desert for nearly two years already. God provided manna for physical sustenance, but manna for breakfast, lunch, and dinner got old really fast.

Listen to the rising tide of complaint as waves of betrayed disappointment flood the camp, spreading from tent to tent — from family to family: "If only we had meat to eat! We remember the fish we ate in Egypt at no cost. . . . Now we have lost our appetite; we never see anything but this manna!" (Numbers 11:4 – 6). Do you hear the Israelites' deep longing for the food of Egypt? This is about more than the actual food. Sure, the manna is getting to them, but they are angry and bitter about their weary existence in the Land Between.

So what comes next? What do the people do — after

witnessing the powerful hand of God demonstrated through the plagues of Egypt, after seeing the waters of the Red Sea part, after being delivered from the armies of Pharaoh, after experiencing God's provision of water in the desert? Not what you think they would. The Israelites succumb to a spirit of complaint, despising God's provision and rejecting his goodness. They actually long for Egypt where they were enslaved!

It's easy to point the finger at the Israelites here. Their attitude toward God gets pretty ugly and ungrateful. But let's consider our reactions for a moment. We, too, can get pretty ugly in our responses to God's provision. I would venture to say most of us are not unacquainted with complaint. It's different when we read about it. When we encounter rebellion like this in Scripture, it's easy to place ourselves *above* the people involved, to view ourselves as superior. We think, "These people are idiots. I would never react like that."

As we walk through this book together, let's try a different approach. Let's try placing ourselves *among* the characters and admit what is true: "Given the right set of circumstances, I might have complained too." For the story to work its intended transformation in our lives, we need to see ourselves as prone to the same weaknesses, capable of the same failings, and tempted by the same sins. It is imperative to associate *with* the characters in the story even when they are misbehaving, rather than placing ourselves above them. What are some ways you can identify with the Israelites' spirit of complaint? When was the last time you felt sick and tired?

An Experiment

I have personally never had to subsist on very limited food choices for any length of time, so a few years ago, when I was preparing to preach a sermon on the Israelites and manna, I decided to try it out for myself—nothing heroic, just a four-day visit to the wilderness of consuming a single menu item. I vowed to dine only on toffee chocolate chip power bars from Tuesday morning to Friday evening. Secretly, I thought this was brilliant. I would have an existential connection with the text that would provide insight and energy for the upcoming sermon.

Here is a record of what happened:

Day 1: Tuesday

Toffee chocolate chip power bar for breakfast. I'm not a huge breakfast person anyway, so this was no big deal.

Toffee chocolate chip power bar for lunch. Not a problem. The experiment was under way.

But arriving home from the office that evening, my wife, Chris, and daughter, Sarah, were cooking. The aroma of the Asian vegetable stir-fry filled the house. I dutifully cut my power bar into five pieces, arranged them neatly on a plate, and took my place at the table. This was not going to be a challenge. I am a disciplined man.

Day 2: Wednesday

Toffee chocolate chip power bar for breakfast.

I arrived midday at the church offices for our weekly senior staff meeting. We have a ritual of bringing our lunches and eating together before we discuss church business. As I walked into the conference room, I sensed a powerful presence. Boxes of pizza beckoned from the conference table, leftovers from the meeting that preceded ours. "Help yourself," someone offered. I cheerfully declined as I surveyed the boxes, mentally noting the ingredients — mushrooms, sausage, pepperoni.

That evening, I arrived home for "dinner," and thankfully the house was empty. At least that night my resolve would not have to compete with a family dining experience. I chewed on my toffee chocolate chip power bar as I sat down to read the newspaper. An advertisement from Taco Bell fell from the pages. Retrieving the colorful ad, I surveyed the pictures on the coupons. I was beginning to cultivate a rich fantasy life.

Day 3: Thursday

Toffee chocolate chip power bar for breakfast and lunch.

As I drove back to the office after a lunchtime jog, I was struck by the fragrance of the Chinese buffet I passed on Cascade Road.

Thursday evening the kids had friends over, and dinner was being served outside on our deck. A delicious pasta salad waited on the table. Burgers and bratwurst sizzled on the grill. Surrounded by this bounty of texture and flavor, smitten by the options, I unwrapped my unappetizing meal from its lousy wrapper. I was starting to rethink this experiment. Seated behind a lovely plate of food, Sarah, who was taking great delight in my misery, needled: "Come on, Dad, join us. You can just tell the congregation you cracked after three days." To my dearly beloved firstborn child, I whispered, "Get thee behind me, Satan."

Confession time: I cheated. Not a total breakdown of my resolve, but I covertly sneaked four lovely potato chips and illicitly tasted a delectable forkful of pasta salad. I was cracking.

Day 4: Friday

Friday was going to be an easy day because I knew the finish line was in sight. My fast would end that evening. For breakfast I crumbled two nauseating power bars into a bowl and soaked them with warm milk in an attempt to trick them into thinking they were cereal.

At lunch I opened one last oppressive wrapper and forced down a final toffee chocolate chip power bar.

Friday evening, having endured my four-day wilderness experiment, Chris and I shared a glorious picnic beside a stream near our home. We devoured crisp crackers, imported cheese, and thinly sliced salami. I wish I could report that the post–power bar picnic was the most delicious meal of my life, but truthfully, this meal was simply not as good as one more toffee chocolate chip power bar would have been bad. I have never eaten another.

.....

Now you might be thinking, at least in the wilderness the children of the exodus didn't have the competing aromas of vegetable stir-fry or the sound of sizzling hamburgers. Fortunately, they didn't endure the experience of piping hot pizza being delivered to their neighbors as they dished up yet another spoonful of boiled manna mush for their kids. But the former slaves did have their memories — memories of the food that flourished in abundance in the lush Nile Delta. In their complaint, these memories are itemized in a grocery list of foods they used to find available in abundance: "We remember the fish we ate in Egypt at no cost — also the cucumbers, melons, leeks, onions and garlic" (Numbers 11:5).

Active memories conjure up visions of meals past, and as a parade of ingredients passes through their minds, they recall the flavor, the aroma, the texture — but mostly the variety. "Now all we have is this manna!" they cry. Bland sameness meal after meal. Boil it, broil it, bake it, or sauté it, the joy has evaporated from the dining experience.

During my four-day experiment, I learned some things

about my relationship with food. I discovered that I enjoy asking the question "What's for dinner?" when I am likely to experience some level of surprise at the answer. During the power bar experience, I lost the joy of anticipating food. I also lost the pleasure of eating. I was hungry and ate, but eating became a joyless function. I gained new appreciation for the Israelites' complaint: "We have lost our appetite; we never see anything but this manna!" (Numbers 11:6).

I'm Sick of This!

Let's go back to considering our own lives. As you journey through the Land Between, what is wearing you out? What is eroding your energy and draining your joy? Consider the frustrated complaint spreading from tent to tent in the wilderness: "We're sick of this!" As you hear the voices swell into a choir of the discontented, is it possible that your own voice is rising with theirs? "I'm sick of this!" As we grow sick of our situation, weary of the Land Between, where might frustration be morphing into the spirit of complaint and taking up residence in your heart?

"I'm sick of living in my in-laws' basement."

"I'm sick of being asked what line of work I'm in and fumbling for an answer."

"I'm sick of enduring wave after wave of medical tests without a clear diagnosis."

"I'm sick of waiting for this depression to lift."

"I'm sick of visiting a mother in a nursing home who repeatedly asks who I am."

"I'm sick of this manna!"

We may think that nothing grows in the desert. But make no mistake: the Land Between is fertile ground for complaint. At face value, complaining doesn't seem like much of a crime — surely it must fall into the misdemeanor category. But as we read a little further in the story of the Israelites, we see that God takes the business of complaining very seriously. To God the Israelites' complaints amount to a rejection of him. He says, "You have rejected the LORD, who is among you, and have wailed before him, saying, 'Why did we ever leave Egypt?'" (Numbers 11:20).

God's evaluation of the situation constitutes a critical development in the narrative. Apparently the Israelites were not merely griping about the food; they were complaining against God. They were not simply rejecting the food; they were rejecting their God. Their complaint about manna accompanied with their longing for Egypt implied, "God, we were better off in Egypt. We were better off without you." Something in their complaint bordered on cosmic treason.

This was indeed a very grave situation. Jacob's sons and daughters were demonstrating a stunning lack of trust. And after all God had done for them! Once again we can get on the bandwagon of condemning the Israelites, but if we desire God's Word to achieve its transforming work in our lives, we must look within and ask the probing questions: "Where do I do this? When is my heart drawn to bitter complaint? In this complaint, is there any possibility I might be guilty of implying, 'God, I was better off without you'?"

As we will see, there is a difference between complaint and an honest expression of our feelings before God. God invites us to be honest. Honesty with God is productive and healing. But there can be a fine line between honesty and complaint, and when traveling through the Land Between, we need to recognize that our souls are very vulnerable. The Land Between may provide our greatest opportunity for transformational growth, but it also provides an enormous opportunity for bitter resentments to flourish — for faith to shrivel.

CHAPTER 2

REPEAT OFFENDERS

WE AGREED TO MEET AT 10:00 p.m. at Denny's, where we figured we could find a quiet corner for an intensely personal conversation. When I arrived, Tony had already secured a booth and was cradling a mug of coffee. His wife — soon to be ex-wife — had moved out, announced that she had no interest in counseling or reconciliation, and left the state to join the man who had stolen her heart. It seemed that the only remaining conversation was who was going to get what.

Tony quickly realized that with only one income, he could no longer make the mortgage payment on their — his — home and would soon be looking for an apartment. He spoke bitterly of the prospects of selling the house in a down market, projecting the beating he would take on the sale. He was certain that he would realize no equity after all those years of making payments. Foremost in the ongoing conflict was who would end up with the newer car and who would have to drive the beater. The quibbling extended to the appliances—not only who would take possession of the washer and dryer, but trivial stuff such as the toaster and the blender.

It was tragic to me that Tony was losing his wife, and here we were in a Denny's talking about losing the toaster. As he spoke about the division of the household items, his energy level began to elevate and the intensity picked up. Customers at nearby tables began to look over nervously as his voice got louder. I could feel his deep disappointment transition into a fuming anger, which in part I found excusable, understandable. But as he vented, I could sense something inside him turning a deep shade of bitter.

As I sat opposite Tony in the booth, I realized that in fifteen years, neither of them would be driving either car. Both vehicles would be on a scrap heap somewhere. The washer and dryer would be history. The toaster would be long gone, experiencing a much shorter life span. But the decisions of the heart made in this troubled space could affect Tony's life fifteen years later. Certainly he would need to walk through stages of emotion, stages of grief, as he worked to process the betrayal, heartache, and loss. But habits of the heart and patterns of response can also take hold during times of challenge—in the Land Between. I realized as we sat together in the late hours in a half-empty restaurant that Tony was in the process of deciding who he was becoming. I was shaken by the reality that his response to the divorce could end up having a greater effect on his life than the divorce itself.

As we pass through the Land Between, it is critical to recognize that not simply the hardship, but also our reaction to the hardship, is forming us. With each discomfort we experience, our responses both reveal the person we are and set the trajectory for the person we are becoming. Whether we age with grace and poise or become bitter, resentful people is largely determined by our response to disappointment and the *habits* of response that often result.

Murmuring

As the Israelites travel through the desert, they demonstrate an entrenched, habitual response to hardship — the people "murmur" repeatedly when they encounter harsh conditions.

It is important to understand that the complaints about manna did not represent the first time the Israelites had reacted this way. They had been in the desert for almost two years and had produced a litany of complaints in a number of contrary moments. From the outset of the journey, grumbling had been a hallmark of their relationship with God.

Though complaint may seem relatively benign when compared with other kinds of responses, its compounded effects can prove profoundly tragic. Through choosing to complain, the Israelites forfeit the opportunity to become a people of faith. With each difficulty, God is whispering, "Will you trust me?" With each collective complaint, they yell, "No, we will not!"

Let's take a look at three earlier wilderness events that provide important insight into the engrained habits of the people and offer a backdrop for the manna episode. In each of these stories there is a repeated sequence. Note the harsh circumstances, the response of grumbling, and finally, God's provision, which factor into each of our three episodes.

Water: Exodus 15

As soon as the Israelites exit dramatically out of Egypt and enter the wilderness, they experience a water crisis. They journey three nasty, hot, dehydrating days without finding water and find themselves in a life-and-death situation.

Finally, when water is located, their relief turns to despair as they discover the water is undrinkable because it is bitter. We read that the people demand of Moses, "What are we to drink?" (v. 24). The complaint is against Moses, God's appointed and anointed leader.

Keep in mind, water is a basic need. This is not grumbling because our flight has been delayed ninety minutes or because our steak has arrived slightly undercooked. We are talking water here. Imagine crying children and fainting grandparents. Three days have gone by with no water—that seems like a pretty harsh situation—and the sons and daughters of Jacob respond by grumbling.

In response, the Lord instructs Moses to toss a tree branch into the pool of bitter water. The besieged leader complies, and the water becomes drinkable. God provides water. God provides life. After all, God is life. What if they are supposed to be learning that God can bring something sweet from something rancid — life from death? This new generation is placed in a situation where they are living the story of redemption firsthand.

Food: Exodus 16

After the bitter water incident, the next chapter in Exodus offers a parallel story. This time the crisis is over food, another basic life need. Here the whole community grumbles against Moses, asserting their wish to have died in Egypt where at least they sat around pots of meat and ate all the food they wanted. They accuse Moses of leading them into the desert so they could starve to death.

Again the Israelites are dealing with a basic need — food. The grumbling is not erupting over a golf outing getting rained out or an interminably long checkout line at the grocery store. The Israelites have no food. And again I imagine crying children and fainting grandparents.

This time the grumbling is articulate. It focuses on the abundance of food in Egypt. The Israelites express their preference to have died there rather than in the desert. Conveniently, they overlook the small detail that in Egypt they had been Pharaoh's slave labor force and that their lives had been unbearable. The sense seems to be that they would rather have died in misery in Egypt than in misery in the wilderness.

The Lord provides for this basic food need through the introduction of manna. Later quail are sent as a source of meat. Once again God demonstrates that he is a capable provider for his people. What is he attempting to teach them as he leads them into dire hardship? "I am worthy of your trust. You need to learn to depend on me."

Are you detecting a repeated pattern, a rhythm in this wilderness song? A crisis occurs over a basic need, the people grumble, and God provides.

Water Again: Exodus 17

Yet another incident occurs in the very next chapter. Here the Israelites encounter a second water crisis. Beneath the scorching sun of the wilderness, they again raise their parched voices against Moses. Scripture says, "The whole Israelite community set out from the Desert of Sin, traveling from place to place as the LORD commanded. They camped at Rephidim, but there was no water for the people to drink. So they quarreled with Moses and said, 'Give us water to drink.'

"Moses replied, 'Why do you quarrel with me? Why do you put the LORD to the test?'" (vv. 1–2).

God instructs Moses to strike a large rock with his shepherd's staff. God's provision is utterly remarkable as water gushes from a rock. A rock is a dead thing, and water is life. Life from nonlife. Water from nowhere, from nothing. Life out of death.

But in this final episode, Moses reacts to the people with the accusation, "Why do you put the LORD to the test?" There is something about perpetual grumbling in the context of faithful provision that constitutes flirting with disaster. God is clearly after something that the people are missing.

What is he doing? My suspicion is that God is leading them into life-threatening situations to prove that he can be trusted. But the Israelites continue to respond in doubt. They keep complaining. Murmuring becomes a repeating pattern. Note again the cycle: a crisis, grumbling, and God's provision. The people are supposed to be learning trust along the way, but it appears their experiences are going wasted.

Let's consider again that the Land Between and its hardships are meant to train and transform the people. God's intent is to use the harsh conditions of the wilderness to prove his faithfulness. If these faith lessons take hold, then the people will be molded into a people of trust, prepared to enter the land promised to their ancestors. Do you see that? The Land Between and its hardships are meant to get them ready for the Promised Land. The question being asked of them through these trials is "Who is the source of life? Upon whom will you depend for water, food, and survival?" Once they enter the Promised Land, they are going to have to resist looking to the likes of the god Baal for water, food, and survival. Dependence on God will be vital, and the desert is a training ground for that dependence. Hear the whisper of their Creator: "I am all sufficient. Turn to me. Trust me. I am proving myself as a capable provider."

Judging by the Israelites' repeating pattern of complaint, it seems the desert training isn't kicking in. What is evident is that these people have a propensity to gripe when they feel their lives are threatened. I am not speaking of the Israelites dismissively here. I am pointing out their pattern of response so that we can hold it up as a mirror to our own. How do you and I respond in harsh circumstances? Do we do any better? Do we trust? Do we respond in faith? Are we allowing ourselves to be disciplined and trained by the hardships we experience in the Land Between so that we can live in greater dependence on God? Remember, our patterns of response to our challenges and trials will shape who we become.

CHAPTER 3

THE JOURNEY OF TRUST

JULIE AND HER HUSBAND, CHRIS, LIVE in Bradenton, Florida, and have traveled through a heartrending wilderness of infertility. The birth of their daughter, Olivia, came after a lengthy process involving surgery and in vitro fertilization. Then came a sequence of three miscarriages as they attempted to have a second child. After the third miscarriage, Julie's deep sorrow turned in the direction of resentful anger. The feelings of loss and frustration were compounded by the fact that her sister was pregnant at the time and Julie needed to offer halfhearted support at a series of baby showers. She was angry, depressed, and mad at God. Why was this happening to her, and why was God allowing this? She was utterly miserable and dreading the pity she would receive at the baby showers, and she shuddered at the prospect of the "I'm sorry, you broken and damaged person" looks she suspected would be cast her way.

God then used a sermon on choosing joy to help Julie heal. She absorbed the reality that it is not a matter of "if" bad things will happen but "when." She would not always have a choice in what would happen, but she did have a choice in her response. Julie decided to allow her painful situation to result in deepening faith that would draw her closer to God. She began to desire a growing faith that emerges from deep suffering. She also chose to rely on God's timing in the gift of another child, trusting that God was at work in her situation.

Though Julie experienced an enormous spiritual breakthrough, the heartbreak did not end. The decision to trust God, to choose joy in the suffering, did not reverse Julie and Chris's situation. In the months following the baby shower, they again embraced the grieving process as they endured two more miscarriages. During these dark days, Julie chose to lean into God and to allow friends and family to reach out to them in a way she had not been able to handle previously. Julie reaffirmed her commitment to choose joy even with an aching heart.

Sometime later, fifteen months after deciding to completely trust God, Julie gave birth to a beautiful baby girl. They named their daughter Ellie Joy. The true miracle of the story is not simply that God has blessed Julie and Chris with a second daughter. The wonder is that their faith flourished in the middle of a mess. While others may have responded by becoming hardened or embittered, Julie chose to trust God through this painful time. She chose to wait upon God's timing for a second child and to choose joy in a season of intense pain.

The Story of Abraham

The Israelites in the desert held a valuable commodity. They possessed the story of Abraham, the father of their people. Abraham's story was a journey of trust that could have guided them through the trauma of the Land Between. As they left Egypt and journeyed into the wilderness, the Israelites carried with them a legacy of God's care and provision for Abraham — and a legacy of Abraham's faith.

The story of the exodus begins when the Lord recruits Moses at the burning bush to lead the people out of slavery, identifying himself as "the God of Abraham, the God of Isaac and the God of Jacob" (Exodus 3:6), the Israelites' forefathers. When God says that he will take them out of Egypt and lead them to the land he promised on oath to their forefathers, he is speaking words that Moses can understand. Moses and the Israelites knew the history of their forefathers. Abraham was not a distant, unknown, ancestor. The Israelites were fully acquainted with his journey of trust — a journey that should have influenced their own behavior.

The story of Abraham begins and ends with the question, "Will you trust me?" God asked a man in the Persian Gulf region to leave his country, family, and culture and to move to an unknown land, a land he had never seen. God said, "I will make you into a great nation and I will bless you; I will make your name great, and you will be a blessing. I will bless those who bless you, and whoever curses you I will curse; and all peoples on earth will be blessed through you" (Genesis 12:2–3).

God has one small prerequisite to this unbelievable outpouring of blessing: "Trust me completely." Abraham is commanded to leave comfort and familiarity and safety. "I need you to trust me. If you do this, I will bless you and bless the world through you."

And Abraham does it. He takes God up on his offer, packs his stuff, and heads to Canaan with Sarah, his infertile wife, to start a nation. Abraham and Sarah are old — way past childbearing years — but they move into the unknown based on God's promise "Trust me, and I will bless you."

The Israelites in the wilderness knew this story. They knew the details of Abraham's journey, which began with a command and a promise. "Leave and I will bless you. Leave everything familiar — your country, your customs, your people — and move to a land that I will show you." They knew that God had called Abraham and that Abraham had followed. This was the Israelites' story.

Abraham enters his own Land Between as he strikes out into the unknown, discovering the God whose voice was demanding yet promising so much. When I read the story, what I anticipate next is that blessing will be dumped on this faithful pilgrim. After all, that was the deal. "Move to the place I will show you, and I will pour out my blessing on you in unimaginable ways." Instead, the story takes a sudden, demoralizing twist. We read, "Now there was a famine in the land" (Genesis 12:10). Abraham obediently, faithfully, moves as God has told him, and what does he encounter but scarcity? I'm guessing this is not the blessing Abraham was in search of when he followed God's voice and left home.

In addition, becoming a nation as God had promised depended on Abraham's having children, and he and Sarah remained childless even as they continued to age. Time was slipping away. No pregnancy, no child, no heir, no nation. Childless and waiting, Abraham is swept up into a regional war in which he and his allies defeat an alliance of kings from the north. Upon returning home, Abraham is met by Melchizedek, king of Salem. Melchizedek is described as a priest of God Most High. He comes out to meet Abraham, offering hospitality with a presentation of bread and wine. Then his voice utters these words: "Blessed be Abram by God Most High, Creator of heaven and earth" (Genesis 14:19).

I wonder what impact this blessing had on Abraham, who had moved to this land in response to a promised blessing: "Move and I will bless you." He had moved in response to a promise and was still waiting for the promise to be fulfilled. Now he hears the blessing repeated, mediated through

Melchizedek, the priest-king. The words must have come as incredible relief to Abraham. What an encouragement for him to trust — and to keep trusting. To hear that he and his barren wife were not forgotten.

"Abraham, you have entered into an alliance with God, and he with you. He told you to move and he would bless you. He is the source of life, and he is with you. Abraham, God Most High called you from your homeland and directed you to move. You're still waiting for a child of your own, but he is faithful. Abraham, his blessing is with you."

After numerous twists and turns in their story, Abraham and Sarah finally have a son, whom they name Isaac. All the promises given to Abraham will now be transmitted to Isaac, the child of promise, but Abraham must pass through one more dramatic, climactic faith test: the Lord asks him to sacrifice his son.

At the beginning of the story, Abraham was asked to trust God by letting go of his past — by moving away from his people and his country. Now, near the end of his journey, Abraham is asked to trust God by letting go of his future — releasing his beloved son Isaac through whom the promised blessing is to be fulfilled. In Genesis 22 we read of how Abraham responds in obedient trust to this command to sacrifice his son and then of how God provides a substitute sacrifice in Isaac's place. God says, "Now I know that you fear God, because you have not withheld from me your son, your only son" (v. 12). Abraham comes to know God as the God who provides.

What is critical to remember is that the Israelites traveling through the desert knew these stories. Abraham was the father of their people, and his journey of trust was their spiritual inheritance. The tragedy is that they failed to apply the principles Abraham learned. They "knew" of God's faithfulness but failed to apply this knowledge to their trying situation. In the wilderness, as they encountered difficulty, they had an extraordinary opportunity to experience the goodness of God firsthand — to apply the story of Abraham to their own story and to trust as he had trusted. But instead of cultivating the life of trust, they responded with perpetual grumbling and complaint. Their spiritual endowment was being wasted. Either they lost their history or simply failed to see how it applied.

How are we doing in our Land Between? What kind of response are we cultivating? We, too, have Abraham's story as a touchstone. We also have the story of the Israelites. How will we allow God's movement in the past to encourage obedience in the present?

Our Reaction

We don't always get to choose what happens to us. Often we have no control over what someone does to us — a boss, a spouse, a child, a distracted motorist, a dishonest business partner. But we do have control over our reaction. And we *will* choose something.

We may choose to withdraw emotionally and silently sink into depression. We may choose seething rage — volcanic anger boiling just beneath the surface of our lives. We may choose retail therapy, numbing our disappointment by stuffing an already full closet. We may allow revenge fantasies to consume our days. But we will choose something. We always respond when we experience deep disappointment. The only question is *how* we will respond.

Sometimes our decisions don't feel like choices. It is possible to select a destructive response so frequently that it no longer feels like a decision. It has become a pattern like the Israelites' murmuring. We respond with a damaging reaction so habitually that it becomes an automatic reflex to a disappointing event.

Don't be fooled. We choose. We will respond to painful situations, and the choice of response is ours.

That choice is an opportunity. When we experience severe hardship, our faith is being tested — just as Abraham's faith was tested when God told him to leave his home and to sacrifice Isaac. Our faith is tested for our good. God allowed the Israelites to endure hardship in the desert so he could provide for them, so they would learn trust and dependence. The writer James encouraged the young Christians of the early church by reminding them that "the testing of your faith" develops perseverance (1:3). This is critical. When things begin to spin out of control, our faith comes under fire. If we can choose to trust God, then we will develop perseverance and faith will grow. We will grow.

There is something about enduring a season of unremitting difficulty that is faith clarifying. The question before us is this: Will we endure this trial (fill in the blank: unemployment, infertility, runaway teenager or runaway spouse, unexplained depression, humiliating financial setback) and still possess a faith that is alive and well? Will we pass through this vast disappointment and still cling to the belief that God is good, that God is wise, that God is loving? Will we trust God? Or will our faith in a good, wise, and loving God evaporate as our patience grows thin and our spirits tire?

The heart drifts toward complaint as if by gravitational pull — after all, complaint seems a reasonable response to a sequence of disappointing events. Generally, you don't have to extend an invitation for complaint to show up. It arrives as an uninvited guest. You return home from yet another frustrating day to discover that complaint has moved into your guest room, unpacked its luggage, started a load of laundry, and is rooting through your fridge. Even as you seek to dislodge complaint — as you move its bags to the curb and change the locks — it crawls back through the guest room window. Complaint resists eviction.

Before we know it, complaint feels right because it is

familiar. With every struggle, we become the Israelites murmuring in the desert. We miss the faith lessons. God desires to prepare us and build things into us, but we are hunkered down in our pattern of response. We need to wake up and notice what is happening! How do we evict that spirit of complaint?

I have heard it said that "bad movement pushes out good movement" and "good movement pushes out bad movement." We can discourage complaint's residency in our lives by inviting another guest to move in with us. That new guest is trust. When we choose to trust in the face of deep disappointment, complaint has less space to maneuver. While attempting to unpack for an extended stay, it discovers that trust has taken all the drawers in the guest room and already occupies the empty seat at the table. Trust evicts complaint. Trust and complaint are incompatible roommates. One inevitably pushes the other one out.

PART 2

MELTDOWN

CHAPTER 4

THE WEIGHT OF DISCOURAGEMENT

THE SUMMER BEFORE MY SENIOR YEAR of Bible college, I began preaching at Ada Bible Church near Grand Rapids, Michigan. I was twenty-one and newly married. The church was in transition, having lost the church planter who began the ministry seven years earlier. Weekly attendance ranged in the midtwenties with half a dozen faithful families holding things together. I was paid twenty-five dollars per sermon. Most of them were worth it.

Ada Bible Church met in a building that was designed to be converted into a three-bedroom house. The sanctuary, twenty-four feet in width, would become a two-stall garage. It was a humble start. But as months passed, we began to grow as college students and young families made our church their home.

To the left of the pulpit hung an attendance board—the kind with numbers that slide into grooves—announcing the attendance and the offering from the previous weekend. The board also displayed the record attendance. We watched the numbers move upward, the record attendance moving through the sixties and seventies and finally to over a hundred. With the advent of the megachurch, I realize this growth may seem unremarkable, but trust me, watching the numbers climb upward was intoxicating. There was a sensation of forward motion, like that of a train moving toward a destination. We were going places, and each month brought new people who wanted to be part of a dynamic ministry.

As our small building filled with new faces, we knew we needed to build something larger. The church had purchased property, and we began conversations on the size, scope, and layout of our new facility. I announced to the congregation that we would break ground the following April. We were building!

On icy days, when I walk to the mailbox out on the road, I can often detect the distinct scent of wood smoke from a neighbor's wood-burning stove. Growth, too, has an aroma. When there is momentum, you can smell it in the air.

But as April approached, it became evident that we were nowhere close to being ready. On a Sunday morning before my sermon, I announced that we were delaying the project a year. I explained that it would be better to postpone our building program rather than rush into it without adequate preparation.

People thanked me. We could endure our modest structure for another twelve months.

As the next spring approached, however, a manufacturing company expressed interest in buying our land. This prompted a new series of conversations as we explored alternative locations. As weeks of indecision drifted into months, I found myself again making an announcement to the congregation before a Sunday sermon. I explained our situation, gave the reasons behind yet another delay, and issued promises that we would build the following year. I don't remember anyone thanking me after this announcement.

The next winter, I would make a similar announcement. Three false starts. Three delays. Three years of spinning our wheels, trying to gain sufficient financial traction to move ahead. During this time, the numbers on the attendance board to the left of the pulpit continued to move—but now in the wrong direction. The record attendance number remained the same: 117. But the weekly attendance began to drop through the nineties and seventies, coming to rest in the fifties.

As the attendance board chronicled our story, there was an increased burden on those who remained. The financial load now rested on fewer shoulders. The weight of cleaning the church, mowing the lawn, and guarding the nursery grew heavier as chairs emptied. I remember the shame—not from lower numbers but a shame that accompanied losing families, individuals. These were not just numbers we were losing.

These were families we had served with, laughed with, prayed with, and cried with.

The scenario became familiar. A husband would phone, asking to meet me for coffee. He would explain that his family had begun looking for another church (other churches are not in short supply in Grand Rapids). Several times the departing person would attempt to rescue my emotions with the words, "It's not you — we just need something different." These words always left me feeling like I was being broken up with.

When a family moved on, it wasn't the kind of thing we would run in our church bulletin. "The Weavers don't go here anymore." Instead, before or after a service, someone would remark, "Hey, I haven't seen Bill and Donna around." And I would respond, "Yeah, they've been looking around for another church. They felt it was time to find something different." Conversations like this were multiplied dozens of times over as we lost people. The shame intensified with each conversation.

Decline also has an aroma. When things are regressing, you can smell it in the air. Men and women enter ministry for various reasons. "Because I want to be a deep disappointment to others as well as to myself" is rarely listed among them. I was slowly dying. The coroner's report would declare, "Death by humiliation."

These events took place more than twenty years ago, but the simple exercise of writing about them leaves me feeling tired. As I relive these memories, I feel as though I need a nap. Traveling through the Land Between, we often have to battle discouragement. Sometimes deep discouragement. The wilderness is a place where even the most hopeful must fend off feelings of impatience, futility, or despair.

In my seventh year as pastor of Ada Bible Church, after three years of delays and a year of construction, we finally moved into our new building, an unremarkable structure built with volunteer labor. No attendance board hung in our new facility, but on opening Sunday about a hundred worshipers met to begin this new leg of our journey. We were deeply thankful simply to be where we had been four years before—before the Land Between.

The Edge of Emotional Collapse

As the drama unfolds back in the desert, the complaint about manna intensifies into exasperated rage. The grievance spreads through the camp and boils over into a furious demand: "Give us meat to eat!" (Numbers 11:13). The complaint is directed toward Moses. As we check in on our besieged leader, remember Moses didn't want this job to begin with. When as a shepherd he had been recruited to lead the people out of slavery, he protested vehemently, feeling totally inadequate for the task. Now, with a near riot on his hands, it is clear that Moses is at a breaking point, utterly incapable of meeting the people's demand. Numbers 11 records his prayer, which is notable for its unrestrained honesty. As we listen to his cry, we encounter someone who is awfully close to the edge of an emotional collapse.

"Why have you brought this trouble on your servant? What have I done to displease you that you put the burden of all these people on me? Did I conceive all these people? Did I give them birth? Why do you tell me to carry them in my arms, as a nurse carries an infant, to the land you promised on oath to their forefathers? Where can I get meat for all these people? They keep wailing to me, 'Give us meat to eat!' I cannot carry all these people by myself; the burden is too heavy for me. If this is how you are going to treat me, put me to death right now — if I have found favor in your eyes — and do not let me face my own ruin." (Numbers 11:11 – 15)

Moses erupts with an exhausted rant. He fires questions at God about the unreasonable demands of the assignment he has been given. He asserts his utter inability to carry this enormous weight any further. Moses is so discouraged and weary that he asks to die rather than continue on like this. The Land Between is fertile ground for emotional collapse.

Did you notice how much of Moses' prayer is made up of questions? I count six of them. "Why? What have I done to deserve this? How can I do what they're asking? Why? *Why?*"

This sounds more like an exasperated meltdown than a prayer. You might say it sounds a little like the complaining Israelites in some respects—the despair, the frustration, the giving up, Moses' dismissal of his calling, the reference to death. But there is a key difference: Moses' attitude toward God. The Israelites are complaining *about* God. Moses is praying *to* God, and this is a huge distinction. Moses isn't disdainfully rejecting God here. In bringing his questions, he has turned *toward* God. He is not spiraling into spiteful complaint but is candidly pouring his heart out to God. He has maxed out and is in over his head. He is running on fumes. Have you felt this way before? Exasperated and at the end of yourself?

At a complete loss, Moses responds by laying his heart bare before God. "I can't do this!" He uses the parental imagery of conception, birth, and childcare to describe the exhausting role God has given him. In effect, he is saying: "I didn't go into a delivery room and give birth to all these babies! I'm not their parent, and I shouldn't have to carry them across the desert!"

In his depleted condition, Moses feels as if he is carrying an impossible weight. "I cannot carry all these people by myself; the burden is too heavy for me." His arm muscles cramp, his fingers grow numb, the situation begins to slip from his grasp. Moses is losing his grip.

Moses' spirit is broken as he groans, "I can't carry this anymore; it's just too heavy for me." As you eavesdrop on his painful prayer, can you hear other voices? Do you hear the groans of friends whose arms grow weary from the weight they are carrying? Can you recognize your own voice in Moses' words? I can certainly hear my voice. It is the honest cry of the overwhelmed: "I can't carry this anymore. It's too heavy for me."

Too Heavy

Fourteen-year-old Becky slowly walks home from the bus stop, opens the front door, and immediately senses conflict. As she picks up her pace to the refuge of her bedroom, she hears a sniping comment and a degrading reply. This year brought about a new stepfather, complete with a move to a different town and adjustment to a new school. The argument picks up speed with hurtful accusations and slamming doors. She puts on her headphones and turns up the volume on her iPod to drown out the fight, which will conclude predictably with someone storming out of the house and peeling out of the driveway. If this marriage continues to unravel, will it bring a move to yet another town and adjustment to another school?

From the turmoil of Becky's home, can you hear an echo of Moses' prayer? "I can't carry this anymore. It's too heavy for me."

.....

From his cluttered office, Mike spends the afternoon sifting through bills and invoices. The piles of paper tell the story that money is going out much faster than it is coming in. He feels like the captain at the helm of a small boat that is springing leaks more rapidly than he can plug them. He comprehends that the business that took twelve years to build has dissolved in fewer than twelve months. "How much longer can I keep this afloat?" he wonders out loud.

In Mike's discouraged state, listen for the voice of Moses: "It's too heavy, I can't carry this anymore."

.....

The Alzheimer's diagnosis had come two years earlier to Rick's bride of nearly fifty years. He had been trying not to trouble the kids, bearing the burden of Alice's care alone. But then came a truly awful night. Rick was up the entire exhausting, frustrating night in a futile attempt to soothe and settle Alice. In the morning, utterly spent, he picks up the phone to call his son and daughter-in-law to ask for help. Day by day Alice is slipping from him as the disease steals their shared memories. Though she is still living, it feels as if his companion of half a century is gone. With each day, he finds himself more physically and emotionally depleted. "I just don't feel I have the strength for this assignment," he says.

Do you hear the prayer of Moses in Rick's voice? "It's too heavy, I can't carry this anymore."

.....

Something is growing in the desert. Again, the Land Between is fertile ground for emotional collapse. If this term feels exaggerated, then look again at Moses' request near the conclusion of his prayer: "If this is how you are going to treat me, put me to death right now!" Moses asks to die rather than remain under the continued pressure of unbearable leadership.

What burden are you carrying in the desert? What weight of responsibility? What grief? What anxiety, worry, or stress? Perhaps at some point you were sick and tired of it — now you feel nearly crushed under its weight. Discouraged. Unable to keep going — without the motivation to keep going. Let me encourage you. You are not alone. Just like Moses, others have been there at the edge. Many others. We have many precedent-setting stories from history at our fingertips — we need only open the Bible. We have seen how Moses responded in his anguish; now let's witness how other biblical characters turned to God in their pain and misery.

CHAPTER 5

GOOD COMPANY

KIM WORKS ON OUR FACILITIES TEAM at church but has been in Florida recently, assisting her mom who is struggling with Lou Gehrig's disease, or ALS, an incurable, degenerative disease. While away, Kim sent me an email portraying the difficulty of witnessing her mother's suffering. She sees her beautiful mom struggling to breathe — chest rattling from bronchitis, a feeding tube, a neck brace to hold her head up — and having such difficulty speaking that Kim can barely understand her words. But her mom manages a consistent smile even as her body suffers.

Kim wrote of lying in bed at night, listening to the rhythmic sound of the breathing machine, and then of hearing her mom cough and feeling a sudden jolt of fear. Was her mom choking? Could she breathe? Then the God questions came: Why would God allow such a horrid disease to invade her mother's body? What good could possibly come from this?

And then Kim realized that in the darkness of this awful season, she had been crying out to God more than at any other time in her life. She had been calling to him, pleading, opening her heart, pouring out her fears. At the end of her emotional resources, facing a situation utterly out of her control, she had been relying on him as never before.

Biblical Meltdowns

Sometimes we wonder if honesty with God is acceptable. Can we really ask these questions of God? Perhaps we fear that any honest expression of our feelings will put us in the camp with the Israelites and their complaints. That is why the record of Moses' frustrated heart cry is so helpful. Listen again to his exasperation: "What have I done to displease you that you put the burden of all these people on me? . . . I cannot carry all these people by myself; the burden is too heavy for me. If this is how you are going to treat me, put me to death right now — if I have found favor in your eyes — and do not let me face my own ruin" (Numbers 11:11, 14 – 15).

Again, this beleaguered servant is not merely venting about his hardships. He is praying. And in his raw, uninhibited prayer, Moses is facing the right direction. He has begun a conversation with the God of Abraham, the source of life, the one who provides. We, too, can be honest with God. We can ask questions. We can be real and unfiltered. In crying out and expressing our hearts, we are in good company. As noted,

Moses' unrestrained frustration is not the only meltdown in the Bible. He is not the only one to have come unglued before God.

Centuries after the time of Moses, the prophet Elijah experienced a similar moment of desperation. Elijah served God in difficult times. Under the influence of King Ahab and Queen Jezebel, the worship of the god Baal had infected the land of Israel. Elijah's mission was to restore the hearts of the people back to their God. The story reaches a climactic moment with a showdown between Elijah and the prophets of Baal. In a great display, Yahweh, the God of Israel, answers Elijah literally with fire from heaven. The people reaffirm their devotion by chanting, "Yahweh, he is God," and rain falls from the sky, ending a severe drought (1 Kings 18).

At this point in the narrative, we expect grateful euphoria. Elijah, it seems, has completed what he set out to do. Mission accomplished! But right here the story takes a dark turn — Elijah learns that Queen Jezebel plans to kill him. After a great victory, the man of God crumbles emotionally. We read, "Elijah was afraid and ran for his life. . . . He came to a broom tree, sat down under it and prayed that he might die. 'I have had enough, LORD,' he said. 'Take my life; I am no better than my ancestors.' Then he lay down under the tree and fell asleep" (1 Kings 19:3–5).

Did you pay close attention to Elijah's prayer? Does it sound familiar? Maybe a little like Moses' prayer? Maybe something like your own prayers in the Land Between? Elijah tumbles fast—from ecstatic high to depressive low. Like Moses, he is so discouraged that, at least for the moment, death feels preferable to continued futility. He is completely spent, emotionally drained, and feeling as if his life and leadership have been a colossal waste.

Now let's turn to another man in the Bible—Jeremiah, who was commissioned by God to prophesy against the city of Jerusalem before its destruction by the Babylonian army in 586 BC. Jeremiah calls a group of leaders to a valley outside the city and theatrically smashes a clay pot against the rocks. He then gives meaning to this dramatic visual aid by declaring that, like the clay pot, Jerusalem will be utterly ruined. When Jeremiah repeats this sermon in the temple courts, he is arrested, beaten, and placed on public display in stocks, where he remains until morning. The light of day brings Jeremiah's release and his meltdown. Listen to his desperate view of his life and mission.

> Cursed be the day I was born!
>> May the day my mother bore me not be blessed! . . .
> Why did I ever come out of the womb
>> to see trouble and sorrow
>> and to end my days in shame? (Jeremiah 20:14, 18)

Cursing the day he was born reveals Jeremiah's deep despair. Have you ever gotten that low, wishing you had never existed?

Amazingly, Jeremiah precedes this "Why was I even born?" motif with a chorus of heartfelt praise.

> *Sing to the LORD!*
> > *Give praise to the LORD!*
> *He rescues the life of the needy*
> > *from the hands of the wicked. (Jeremiah 20:13)*

These competing responses in Jeremiah's heart were both very sincere. Jeremiah sees the Lord as fully deserving of praise for rescuing him; and yet, humiliated and bleeding, his life is going really badly. He tastes both the goodness of God and the painful brutality of life. The overall effect feels a bit muddled as the two extremes are placed side by side, but as we will see in the next chapter when we look at the Psalms, these extremes coexist throughout the Scriptures — as they do in our own hearts.

Come and Cry Out

What are we to make of the meltdowns of Moses, Elijah, and Jeremiah? As we reflect on their words, it is helpful to consider a couple of things. First, these guys are spiritual heavyweights — heroes of the faith. Though they are flawed human beings, we would not be apt to describe them as spiritually immature. My inclination is that their desperate prayers may be an indication of spiritual health rather than a sign of spiritual deficiency.

Second, in his providence, our Creator chose to include these high-voltage prayers in his Word. God wants us to see them, maybe even to borrow from them, when we find ourselves at a breaking point. Perhaps these prayers and others like them in the Bible were preserved as a way for God to whisper: "See, you're not alone. Some of my choice servants have felt intense failure and frustration. This is how they prayed when they felt empty and exhausted, and this is how I invite you to pray. My shoulders are strong enough to absorb rants like this. But please speak! Cry out! Face me and give voice to your fatigue, your pain, your betrayal, your vast disappointment. Turn toward me and begin the conversation, even if it's raw and ugly."

Could the prayer of Moses provide a vocabulary, a prayer language, for the Land Between? Everything about his prayer feels over the top, but Moses has taken a leap in the right direction by laying his heart open before God. Through his prayer, a conversation is under way.

Centuries after the time of Moses, Jesus would extend the invitation, "Come to me, all you who are weary and burdened, and I will give you rest" (Matthew 11:28). What if Jesus' invitation to the weary and burdened has been on the heart of the Father for all time? Was this the Creator's invitation to Moses? To us? Come and cry out. Come and find rest.

Peter, who walked with Jesus for three years, encouraged those consumed with worry, "Cast all your anxiety on him because he cares for you" (1 Peter 5:7). Here it is God's caring nature that serves as the motivator to cast, or throw, our anxiety toward him.

Look at God's care and concern for his despairing prophet, Elijah. When Elijah is running for his life in mortal fear of Queen Jezebel, he sits down under a broom tree and prays. Remember his words? "I have had enough, LORD," he says. "Take my life; I am no better than my ancestors" (1 Kings 19:4). Then, discouraged and exhausted, he lies down under the shade of the tree and falls asleep. What you might expect next is a lecture, a scolding word from God that Elijah turn around, go back home, and get back to work. Instead, we find a beautiful, unexpected turn in the text: "All at once an angel touched him and said, 'Get up and eat.' He looked around, and there by his head was a cake of bread baked over hot coals, and a jar of water. He ate and drank and then lay down again" (vv. 5–6).

The meal to which Elijah awakens is not day-old, thrift-store bread but bread baking over hot coals. Fresh bread, hot bread. You could smell it baking. Here is Elijah, God's discouraged, exhausted servant, utterly spent, and he wakes to the aroma of hot bread and the refreshment of cool water. Something in this interaction touches me in a very deep place. I am expecting Elijah to receive a rebuke, and instead, God bakes him bread. It's as if God tenderly says: "Dude, you could use some lunch. You must be so tired and so disillusioned.

Here, I've made something just for you. Have some food and get some rest."

God's response to Elijah's cry of despair is tender care. Perhaps our own slowness to pray is anchored in a suspicion that God is somehow unconcerned with us. Our view of God affects whether we will seek him in our hour of crisis. If we view God as distant, removed, and unconcerned, we won't likely turn to him when we feel things spinning out of control. Conversely, if we view him as concerned, present, and caring, we will be significantly more likely to draw near with our need.

CHAPTER 6

THE ART OF CRYING OUT

BILL LOST HIS FATHER TEN YEARS before his father died. Dementia removed him from the family business and confined him to a nursing home. Though still living, his dad was not available to play the role of grandfather to Bill's children. He was not there to witness the company passing into Bill's hands, and he was not there to give desperately needed counsel as the manufacturing industry struggled. Time after time, Bill wished he could talk to his dad and receive guidance in complicated business situations, but instead he was forced to navigate these storms alone.

A simple event brought Bill's loss bubbling to the surface. While he was attempting to sell his house, an interested young couple brought their parents through. Bill observed as the son talked over the potential purchase with his father, and witnessing the interaction, he felt an acute sense of robbery. The more he mused on the simple sight of a son getting advice from his father, the more he felt as if something had been stolen—unfairly taken—from him. A voice inside began to demand, *Where was my dad when I needed him?*

When Bill opened up to me about the incident and the intense sense of loss he was experiencing, it was clear that his wound was not healing. I asked if he had poured out his pain to God, if he had vented to God about how unfair he felt it was that other people get to enjoy the companionship of parents while his dad was torn away. Since the idea felt a little alien to Bill, I encouraged him to take a personal retreat, perhaps to a cottage or cabin somewhere for a couple days. There he could read through the psalms of David, pausing when he found language that matched his grief and longing. Then he could borrow fragments, sentences, and verses and form his own prayer of lament so he could pour out his pain, longing, hurt, and grief and ask God for healing and mercy.

My hope was that Bill might become unstuck—that the healing process might accelerate as he used the Psalms as a guide to form his own lament, his own heart's cry, about losing his dad. When traveling through the Land Between, we can feel that we are carrying unbelievable weight or being ripped apart by forces beyond our control. In our disorientation, it is possible to overlook a basic healing exercise. That exercise is acquainting God with our deep need. Somehow we don't respond to his invitation to come and cry out. We ask, "But if he's God and already knows about our situation, why do we need to inform him?" Because we need to speak. Just as was true with Moses, the very act of voicing our trouble to God begins a conversation in which we have opened ourselves up to his care, his mercy, and his provision.

Let's expand our discussion on Moses' ranting prayer in the desert by venturing into the psalms of David.

The Poetry of Trust

As we have seen, Moses' emotional meltdown in the wilderness results in an exasperated cry to God. Moses reveals the consuming weight of his situation, concluding, "This is too heavy for me. I just can't carry this anymore." This desperate prayer uttered by Moses finds voice in David's psalms. As a young man, David is anointed to be Israel's next king. Soon things begin to unravel as the reigning king, Saul, becomes insanely jealous of David's growing popularity and military success. The ensuing season is riddled with cliff-hangers and close calls as David is stalked by Saul like a hunted animal. David spends years of his life running and hiding.

After Saul's death, when David becomes king, he is plagued by myriad difficulties, perhaps the most painful being a nearly successful coup attempt led by his own son Absalom. David's prayers of desperation are collected in the book of Psalms, where he pours out his heart to God — his anguish and his hope, his despair and his faith. This is the poetry of trust.

Crying out to God is an art form. Or at least it can be. As we scan the Psalms, we may forget that these are song lyrics, written to be sung to musical accompaniment. Many of these songs use the vehicle of artistically crafted poetry to transport the prayers of the weary, exhausted, and betrayed. Frustration is pushed skyward through graphic imagery, metaphor, and rhyme.

Take Psalm 69 as an example. Rather than simply praying, "God, I'm really doing badly and could use some help," King David develops the imagery of drowning to express the panic and utter desperation of his situation.

> *Save me, O God,*
> > *for the waters have come up to my neck.*
> *I sink in the miry depths,*
> > *where there is no foothold.*
> *I have come into the deep waters;*
> > *the floods engulf me. (vv. 1–2)*

In David's song, the waters are rising and he can't find his footing. He begins to sink. Pulled out to sea by difficulty, he screams, "God, I'm drowning here!" Scanning the shore for help, he yells until he is hoarse. No lifeguard is visible. His prayer is the cry of a drowning man.

The power of the poetry is its timelessness. We talk about "drowning in debt" or "being in over our heads" when things are overwhelming. Many know the feeling of being engulfed in waves of grief or swept out to sea by a riptide of disappointment. Later in his song, David will rework the metaphor into his petition for help. "Do not let me sink. Deliver me from those who hate me, from the deep water. Do not let the floodwaters engulf me."

I have a powerful childhood memory, one of only a handful I can summon from my preschool years. I am splashing in the shallow end of a large pool. The diving board is at the opposite end, and beyond that, the building with the changing rooms painted red. I wade toward the rope separating deep from shallow, but the pool bottom slopes downward before the rope and I'm suddenly in over my head. I flail in panic. My dad's friend Ira reaches over and grabs me and pulls me to the side of the pool. I'm confident that Ira has long forgotten this, and I'm equally confident that I never will. I can't think of a stronger metaphor to depict desperation.

King David uses the vehicles of music and poetry to voice both his trouble and his trust. He refuses to diminish the struggle he is experiencing, but he cries out to God to act mercifully on his behalf. Again, this is poetry of trust. These songs remind us that we are not alone in our struggles. Others have gone before us. And the Psalms can guide us in shaping articulate, honest prayers in desperate times. Through them we can express both our trouble and our trust.

Let's look, too, at Psalm 55. Besieged by difficulty and betrayed by a close friend, David borrows the imagery of flight to describe his longing for peace. I imagine the king approaching a window ledge. He startles a nesting dove and then there is an explosion of beating wings as the bird heads toward the desert. David, enveloped in chaos, watches the dove grow smaller and smaller as it disappears on the horizon. He whispers, "I wish I were you." And a song is born.

> *"Oh, that I had the wings of a dove!*
> *I would fly away and be at rest." (v. 6)*

In the poem, David piles up words to describe his miserable condition — "trouble," "distress," "suffering," "anguish," "terrors," "fear," "trembling," and "horror." He is not holding back — like Moses, he is honest, real about his situation and his emotions. Overwhelmed and scared, David longs for rest. "If I could only sprout wings and leave all this mess behind," he groans. Again, the power of the imagery is that it is timeless. In the movie *Forrest Gump*, young Jenny leads Forrest into the cornfield behind the shack where she lives with her abusive father. "Pray with me, Forrest," Jenny pleads, as her drunken dad hollers and searches the field for her. They kneel, and Jenny prays, "Dear God, please make me a bird, so I can fly far, far away."

In the three millennia that have passed since David penned his verse about flying away, God's treasured daughters and beloved sons have endured stresses of a thousand varieties, situations from which they longed for rescue. We wish that we could fly away from our haunted past or from the quicksand of loneliness or from debilitating depression — from our trouble. But look at how the song resolves: David urges the listener, "Cast your cares on the LORD" (v. 22). An act of trust. I believe this is what he has been doing all along in the poem.

Crying Out with the Scriptures

Psalms like those we just looked at translate incoherent groans into articulate prayers. They are at our disposal, and we may borrow their vocabulary, even as we may borrow the language of Moses' prayer, to cry out to God when we lack the strength or creativity to put our deep need into words. There are times when we want to express ourselves to God, but we get waylaid by the complexity of our feelings. Or we feel numb, we feel nothing. We are in distress, but like David we are drowning in it. We have no words. We can turn to the Scriptures.

In 1983 the band U2 began concluding their concerts with the song "40" and with the words "How long to sing this song?" The tune is the tenth and final track on U2's *War* album and is a loose version of Psalm 40 penned by King David. As the song, and the concert, would near its end, the band members would depart the stage one at a time — first Bono, then Adam Clayton, Edge, and finally, Larry Mullen Jr. The singing, however, was not over. With the stage empty, the crowd would continue to chant the refrain, "How long to sing this song? How long to sing this song?" It is a question from the Land Between.

In Psalm 13 the same question falls again and again like a hammer striking a nail. "How long?" David asks repeatedly. "How long will you hide your face from me? How long must I wrestle with my thoughts? . . . How long will my enemy triumph over me?" (vv. 1 – 2). It is the question of those worn out from waiting, of those who feel forgotten, left behind. Have you experienced these feelings? Does your wilderness seem interminable? Do you feel you have nothing to look forward to? Have you asked God, "How long?"

As he waits, David manages to cling to his belief that God is good and that he is present. David confesses:

> *But I trust in your unfailing love;*
>   *my heart rejoices in your salvation.*
> *I will sing to the LORD,*
>   *for he has been good to me. (vv. 5 – 6)*

I think the idea is that hope for the future is anchored in God's goodness to us in the past. God has been faithful before, and he will be faithful again. That is the basis of David's trust. That is our hope. The psalm encourages us to bring our questions, our "How long?" to God. It also encourages us to bring our trust — to remind ourselves of God's unfailing love shown us in the past and to place our trust in that love even now. David's song is not a melody of despair but of hope.

Do you see the difference between the movement of emotion here and the spray of bitter words from the Israelites murmuring in the desert? David expresses his feelings, his hurts, his confusion — but he also expresses a determination to trust. He refuses to diminish the struggle he is experiencing, but he cries out to God to act mercifully on his behalf. Trouble and trust coexist in the hearts of the people we meet in the Bible — David, Jeremiah, and others — even as they coexist in our own hearts.

Turning in God's Direction

When I encouraged my friend Bill, still grieving deeply over his father, to go away for a couple days and spend time in the Psalms, I urged him to look for images, language, and lines that resonated with his experience. I challenged him to borrow from the Psalms to craft his own prayers. As I gave this advice, I offered no guarantees that the exercise would prompt a spiritual or emotional breakthrough. I had a hunch that it would be a good exercise and at least begin the conversation moving in a Godward direction.

Weeks later I bumped into Bill and learned he had taken my advice. He retreated to a cottage and, using the Psalms, crafted his own prayer of hurt and hope, of disappointment and trust. And something powerful happened — not total healing but more rapid healing. Something became unstuck. Turning the pain of the years in God's direction, reliving the layers of grief, and reconfirming his trust and hope that God was faithful proved to be a transforming exercise.

Honest prayer is powerful. Moses prays honestly in the desert when besieged by angry people demanding food that he cannot provide. He simply cannot carry the leadership burden anymore, and he throws his pain toward God. In doing so, as we have noted, he is facing in the right direction. A dialogue has started. Intimacy has deepened. In opening his hands to release his frustration and anxiety, he has also opened his hands to receive God's provision. In our honest prayers, so can we.

PART 3

PROVISION

CHAPTER 7

NO LONGER ALONE

BRENT AND SONIA HAVE BEEN FAMILY friends for more than ten years. They have four children. Kaci, who is seventeen, is severely autistic. She speaks very little but communicates as best she can with a mixture of one-word utterances and some sign language. Kaci is a beautiful girl. She can also be a handful. As a young child, she ate with a frenzy that made scrubbing her and the house a daily routine. She would be in bed by 8:00 p.m. but up for the day at 2:00 a.m. As a teenager, she wears diapers and runs into the street without warning. She hits, kicks, bites, and cries her way through life. Kaci can be a danger to herself and to others.

At times Brent and Sonia's journey can seem taxing and dark, but to observe their family is to witness a dance of grace. They have continually drawn upon God's provision during a season marked by enormous disruption, intense fatigue, and a great deal of crying out to him.

As I listen to them, I witness a constant thread of God's redemptive hope woven through the tapestry of their family life and their experiences with Kaci. The tears and exhaustion over the years have been balanced by the irrepressible presence of God's mercy. God knew the toll that caring for Kaci would take, that often they would be tired, weak, and empty. He has provided mercy on this complicated journey, great love, and the rich gifts that come with the privilege of parenting a special needs child.

Brent and Sonia prayed for Kaci's health, healing, and wholeness, but they also cried out for God's strength — for themselves as parents, and especially for their three other children. Again and again over the years, they have seen evidence of his provision. Their older children could have resisted or rebelled, but God softened their hearts toward Kaci and toward himself. Each of the children can tell a story of a journey with God around Kaci. Their son, Kirk, has a psychology degree and works with special needs students in a high school in Illinois. Erin is finishing her master's degree in social work and works with the special needs population in a Michigan school district. Tori is heading to college next fall with the stated interest of doing something with special needs kids. They all are passionate, vibrant Jesus followers. They have emerged from an upbringing that helped them to turn their urgent questions back on God, and he responded by providing peace and direction.

Brent firmly believes that in giving them Kaci, God also gave them himself. Their experience has been exasperatingly hard at times, and often isolating, but God has met them in their low places, restored joy, and given hope. In the Land Between, God provides.

Spreading Out the Burden

Let's check back in on Moses. The wilderness camp is in an uproar. Sick of the manna diet and recalling the limitless vegetables and fish of Egypt, the people have demanded, "Give us meat to eat!" (Numbers 11:13). Moses, at a breaking point, has cried out to God: "I cannot carry all these people by myself; the burden is too heavy for me." The weight of leadership is more than he can bear. Now we are faced with the question, how will God respond to his weary servant?

I share a hope that God will move toward Moses with understanding and mercy. I hope God provides for the crushing weight Moses is facing. My interest is not only in Moses. I hold the hope that when we, too, are depleted and discouraged, pulled far beyond our resources, God will have a heart to provide for us. Let's listen in as God is responding to Moses: "Bring me seventy of Israel's elders who are known to you as leaders and officials among the people. Have them come to the Tent of Meeting, that they may stand there with you. I will come down and speak with you there, and I will take of the Spirit that is on you and put the Spirit on them. They will help you carry the burden of the people so that you will not have to carry it alone" (Numbers 11:16 – 17).

Do you see that? God is agreeing with Moses. God utilizes the same imagery in his response that Moses used in his meltdown. Moses had moaned, "I cannot carry all these people by myself; the burden is too heavy for me" (Numbers 11:14). Now with a promise to multiply leaders for the people, God says: "They will help you carry the burden of the people so that you will not have to carry it alone." The Lord responds to Moses' desperate plea by saying, "You are right; it is too much for you to bear. And I will provide help so that others will carry the burden with you." God spreads out the burden.

God calls Moses and the elders to come to the Tent of Meeting. This tent, which housed the ark of the covenant — the structure that carried the Ten Commandments — is often referred to as the tabernacle. It was a portable worship space surrounded by the tents of the Israelites and represented the physical presence of God among the people. God instructs Moses to bring seventy elders there, men publicly recognized for their ability to officiate and lead.

Apparently Moses had received a unique endowment of God's Spirit when he was commissioned to lead. As these seventy leaders come and stand with Moses at the tabernacle, God reveals his intention to "come down and speak with" Moses. Then God takes the Spirit that rests upon Moses and distributes the Spirit upon the seventy leaders, resulting in a multiplication of God-empowered leadership. Out of his generous, giving nature, God provides for his discouraged leader and for the people. This should prompt a question for those of us traveling through the Land Between: What if God still does this? What if God loves to provide?

A Whisper from God

My mother died on November 30, which meant that my father lost his wife and that five children under the age of fourteen lost our mom between Thanksgiving and Christmas. The holidays only added weight to our grief.

As Christmas drew near, a big box arrived at our home. The box was filled with individually wrapped Christmas presents from a church in the Midwest that had a connection with our family and was aware of the heartache we were facing. An accompanying note to my father relayed, "Don't worry about Christmas presents for your children this year. We want to take care of their Christmas."

A couple days later, another large box arrived, also containing wrapped Christmas gifts. These also came from a Midwest church, and again a heartfelt message read, "Don't worry about buying your children Christmas presents. Please let us take care of this."

A day or two later, when we received a third cache of gifts, I distinctly remember thinking, *I sure hope these churches don't find out about each other.*

Then we received gifts a few days after Christmas from a fourth congregation. They were greatly apologetic about the presents arriving late, but I was ecstatic! It was as if Christmas wouldn't end that year.

While the gifts did not take away our grief, the arrival of a box and the mercy that motivated the givers were like a whisper from God: "I'm here. I see what you're going through. I know and I care. I haven't forgotten you." We were not suddenly well, and my own turmoil had not dissipated with the arrival of a Nerf football and Hot Wheels cars. Things were still pretty much a mess. But in the mess, God reminded our grieving family that we were not alone.

God's Intimate Concern

They unpack for the third time in as many years. The second floor apartment is congested with moving boxes. This time they have secured a month-to-month lease, deciding not to buy a house if this is simply another brief stopover in a series of all-too-frequent transfers. Tomorrow will begin the litany of phone calls to locate a family doctor, enroll the kids in a new school, and hunt for a church. Pam wearies at the prospect of making friends and wonders if it is worth the trouble. Should she even unpack the box of family pictures? Is it worth the time to hang them up in an attempt to make this feel like home? She hears a knock at the door and finds a new neighbor with a plate of cookies welcoming her to the apartment complex. It's as if God is whispering, "I feel your fatigue, and I am concerned about you."

.....

A woman sits in the waiting room of a counselor's office dreading the emotional surgery that will take place when the door opens and her name is called. She thumbs distractedly through a dated magazine, avoiding eye contact with others. "What if someone recognizes me?" She wonders if the strangers in the room can discern why she is there. The memories and emotions of childhood abuse have been intensifying rather than receding with time. They are clearly affecting intimacy with her husband and blocking any sort of meaningful connection with God. As the door opens and a cheerful voice calls her first name, she sets the magazine down and moves toward healing. Through the words of a skilled counselor, she will hear the words of her heavenly Father who treasures her and loves her dearly: "I care about you deeply. I want you to be whole."

.....

While we are traveling through the Land Between, God may provide badly needed money. But he may also provide contentment to live with joy and laughter while living without the extras. I think God loves providing exactly what we need at exactly the right moment.

He may provide a timely email of encouragement. Or in

the absence of a friend, he may speak into our hearts through a well-timed sermon that addresses our situation with clarity and hope. Suddenly we know that God is speaking directly into our lives.

God may provide strength to patiently care for our children one more hour when we find ourselves at an emotional breaking point. Or he may provide a friend to watch the kids for an afternoon so we can sit and read as we recharge without a preschooler calling for our attention. He may provide peace in a difficult time. Whatever it is, God loves to provide for us — providing is what he does. And he does it with intimate knowledge of who we are and what we need. He is concerned about us. Remember the words of Peter. We cast our cares upon him because he cares for us.

Draw Near

Moses experienced God's tender care in the wilderness. There he was breaking under a load too heavy to carry, and God called him to approach the tabernacle, the tent representing God's presence, to draw near and receive help from God, the grace of additional shoulders to carry the load.

God calls us to draw near, as well. "Come unto me. Cry out. Share your heart. Draw near and let me take care of you. Come and receive." That invitation to draw near to God is our hope — *he* is our hope. We draw near to experience his comfort when we are crushed by loss, his closeness when we feel abandoned, and his slow, sure healing when crippled by grief. He is the God who provides. He knows what we need even when we do not. And he knows how he will provide it.

CHAPTER 8

THE GOD WHO SEES

THE BLACK-AND-WHITE PHOTO WAS TAKEN IN 1961. With low mountains behind them, my father is standing next to my mother, who is holding a baby, my sister, Julie. My dad is in a short-sleeved white shirt and khaki pants. He is skinny. Mom is wearing a dark, patterned, calf-length skirt and white blouse. Julie is just a few months old, her baby face shaded by a sun bonnet. She wears frilly socks and has chunky calves. Since only thirteen months separate her birth from mine, Mom is pregnant with me. She wears glasses and smiles at the camera. My parents look so young. Though he is in his early twenties, my dad could probably pass for a high school senior.

At the time, the church they were planting in southeast Idaho had only two or three families attending and was unable to offer any financial help. They had a tiny apartment, which adjoined the church sanctuary, and their income came from outside missionary support — financial sponsorship from other churches — totaling $150 a month. To say that things were strained financially would be an understatement. These were years of incredible financial scarcity — the Land Between — and also a valuable time to grow in trust. Living by faith was not an abstract concept but a way of life.

About a dozen years ago, my father passed on a story to each of us kids in which he documented an incident from these early days of ministry. His letter came on Valentine's Day, and I suspect he wrote his thoughts down in order to pass on a bit of family history that reflected God's faithfulness in a season of scarcity. These stories tend to get lost over time, and his letter has preserved the event for his children and grandchildren. It is a wonderful story of hospitality, shortage, and provision.

On a beautiful July afternoon, during the difficult period reflected in the photograph, my parents received three visitors — I think they were college students — traveling coast to coast and looking for places to stay along the way. My dad had known two of these kids from his home church in Michigan. My parents were encouraged to have company for a couple days, but they barely had enough food for themselves, much less for guests. They had just been to the store and had purchased some basics, which on this occasion included a large chicken reserved for Sunday dinner. It was two or three days before Sunday when their guests arrived. Dad and Mom privately discussed how they would feed their guests and agreed to use the chicken, but they thought that because it was such a large chicken, they would probably not eat more than half of it. This was a dreadful miscalculation. After dinner, all that was left of the chicken was the carcass. When their guests pulled away from their house, my parents' money was gone and so were their groceries.

My parents were convinced it was always right to show hospitality in every way they could, especially to other believers who were in need of lodging and food. They had done this, but now what would God do? Dad told us how he and Mom prayed together, trusting that the Lord would meet their needs.

The evening of the day their guests departed, they received more visitors. These friends were from the small farming community of Aberdeen, Idaho, not far from my parents' home. Over the years, this couple would become some of their closest friends. As they visited, my folks did not relate their financial circumstances nor the fact that they had shared their last groceries with their guests.

Then, as their friends prepared to leave my parents' tiny apartment, they said, "We would like you to come out to the car. We have a few things from the farm we'd like to leave with you." My parents' friends proceeded to unload the car, and Mom and Dad could barely believe what they were seeing. Somehow the Lord had placed my parents on their friends' hearts that day. They blessed my parents with a hundred pounds of potatoes, fresh garden vegetables, four dozen eggs, and, believe it or not, four chickens larger than the one they had just placed on the table for their guests.

My dad is a bit foggy on the details because the event took place decades before, but he thinks that they also gave them some money to help them make ends meet. Mom and Dad brought these dear folks in on their situation, the recent events, and told them that God had used them to answer their prayer from earlier in the day.

My dad, who was writing down this story, concluded with, "That dear couple has been in heaven now for many years. But that gift, their generosity, and their giving spirit—not just with us but with believers everywhere, will forever live in our minds."

There are times when God allows us—as he did the Israelites, as he did Moses—to suffer need. This need may be physical, emotional, spiritual, material, or relational. Such needs have a tendency either to discourage and debilitate us or to drive us into God's presence where we ask for his guidance and provision. God sees us—everything about us. He knows our need. And he is trustworthy. He wants us to learn to trust him to provide.

"I Have Indeed Seen"

Even before God provided the help Moses needed in the wilderness, Moses was familiar with the caring nature of God. If you will remember, when Moses was first commissioned to return to Egypt and lead the people out of slavery, the God of his fathers spoke to him from the bush that was aflame yet not consumed. In fear Moses hid his face. The presence speaking from the burning bush said, "I am the God of your father, the God of Abraham, the God of Isaac and the God of Jacob" (Exodus 3:6). Then came words expressing the reason God had called Moses — his immense concern and compassion for the children of Jacob, oppressed under the yoke of slavery. God said, "I have indeed seen the misery of my people in Egypt. I have heard them crying out because of their slave drivers, and I am concerned about their suffering" (v. 7).

I wonder if Moses wept at those words. The cries of the people had reached the heart of God, and the Creator was moved. "I have seen. . . . I have heard. . . . I am concerned." I believe these words can land with powerful force when spoken over us in our times of confusion and difficulty. On occasion I have spoken these words over my congregation and asked them to receive them as words coming from their heavenly Father, words addressed to their pain and conflict. "I have seen your misery. I have heard you crying. And I am concerned about your situation."

.....

In the New Testament, Jesus is talking to a crowd of people and asks a question: "Why do you worry about clothes?" (Matthew 6:28). Jesus appeals to the natural surroundings of his teaching setting by using the image of lilies of the field. I imagine Jesus motioning toward wildflowers as he speaks these words: "See how the lilies of the field grow. They do not labor or spin. Yet I tell you that not even Solomon in all his splendor was dressed like one of these. If that is how God clothes the grass of the field, which is here today and tomorrow is thrown into the fire, will he not much more clothe you, O you of little faith?" (vv. 28 – 30).

Jesus contrasts the beauty of the flowers with the opulence of Solomon, son of David, king of Israel. Even with all Solomon's wealth, his royal robes could not compare with the beauty of wildflowers. The king's wardrobe couldn't touch the transcendent beauty of the Creator's landscape. Then he asks a penetrating question: "If that is how God clothes the grass of the field, which is here today and tomorrow is thrown into the fire, will he not much more clothe you, O you of little faith?" (v. 30).

Whatever you are facing — prolonged illness, financial collapse, family pain, career confusion, unexplained depression, aching loss — pause for a moment and hear these words whispered by the Creator into your situation: "Do not worry. I have seen. I have heard. Trust me. Believe in me. I am concerned."

Seeing Us in the Desert

Let's return for a moment to the pilgrimage of Abraham. He and his wife, Sarah, wait to see God's promise fulfilled—a nation coming forth from their own bodies. A decade passes and still no pregnancy, no child for this aging couple now long past childbearing age. After this ten-year wait, geriatric Sarah presents a plan to her octogenarian husband: "Sleep with my maidservant; perhaps I can build a family through her" (Genesis 16:2). This type of surrogate mother arrangement was common in the Middle East. But although it was common in the culture, it appears to have been a breach of trust in God for Abraham and Sarah to pursue this avenue to nation building. We can empathize with Sarah's action. Often when we are tired of waiting, we come up with a plan. Sometimes these plans work out pretty well. Sometimes these plans backfire, making our difficult situation even more complicated, for in our impatience, we have taken matters into our own hands.

The result of Sarah's proposal is stated in the Scriptures in an economy of words: "He slept with Hagar, and she conceived" (Genesis 16:4).

The reader of the Abraham story doesn't have to guess what emotions come to the surface in Hagar's heart when she becomes pregnant. Hagar experiences a change of status when she sleeps with Abraham. Formerly, she was simply Sarah's slave, but now they are sharing the same man. In a sense, Hagar too has become Abraham's wife, which elevates her status. The pregnancy emboldens her to feel superior to Sarah, and this is where the drama accelerates. "When she knew she was pregnant, she began to despise her mistress" (Genesis 16:4). I wonder if Hagar smiled condescendingly at Sarah, as if to say, "I'm pregnant, and you're not. I'm carrying his child—something you've never done."

In the movie *Julie and Julia*, Meryl Streep plays the role of Julia Child. There is a scene in which she and her husband are taking a walk through a tree-lined park in Paris. A couple passes them, walking in the opposite direction, pushing a baby stroller. Julia glances at the stroller, and her cheerful expression suddenly darkens. Her husband takes her hand, already curled in his elbow as they walk, and raises her hand to his lips, kisses her hand, and then lovingly pats it. In seconds, the drama of her infertility has been captured. Without dialogue, the brilliant scene portrays the pang of childlessness and the tender action of a husband to assuage the longing that strikes in unexpected moments.

If subtle reminders of infertility can spark deep emotion, what would Sarah experience when blatantly taunted? Sarah is livid and begins to mistreat Hagar terribly. Hagar flees the situation, running away from her master's household. I find it hard to pick a hero in the story, as they all share in the blame. Hagar is arrogant and belittling, Sarah is cruel, and Abraham is passive. No one is innocent here. This is a huge mess of a situation.

Now here is where the story takes an unexpected turn. As Hagar runs away, I am expecting the camera to focus in on Abraham and Sarah, but instead, the camera follows pregnant Hagar as she flees into the desert. In the narrative that follows, the angel of the Lord finds Hagar near a spring in the desert. The angel announces: "You are now with child and you will have a son. You shall name him Ishmael, for the LORD has heard of your misery" (Genesis 16:11).

The angel informs Hagar that the baby she is carrying is a boy. When he is born, she is to give her son the name Ishmael, which means "God hears." The meaning of this name is explained in the next line. "The LORD has heard of your misery."

"Hagar, God knows about your tears, about your confusion, about the mistreatment you are experiencing at the hands of Sarah. Hagar, God hears."

Then the runaway slave does a strange thing. She names God. "She gave this name to the LORD who spoke to her: 'You are the God who sees me' " (Genesis 16:13).

Who is the God who called Abraham to leave his home, his language, his people, and his country? He is the God who hears. He is the God who sees. He is the God who takes up the cause of the rejected, the unloved, and the mistreated.

As we have noted, the Israelites of the wilderness knew Abraham's history — they knew this story. They knew God had revealed himself to Hagar as "the God who sees." They themselves had benefited from God's provision in the harsh conditions of the Land Between—his provision of a way of escape through the Red Sea, of guidance through a pillar of cloud by day and a pillar of fire by night, of food, of water. Even Moses, their deliverer, their leader, was the proof that God saw them—that he had heard their cry as slaves in Egypt. The Israelites had experienced God as the God who sees, but unlike Moses, somehow in their hearts they couldn't hold on to the truth of God's identity. They couldn't *trust* him as the God who sees, the God who provides, the God who cares and loves and is concerned.

In the Land Between, we often feel left to fend for ourselves. We feel wretched, beat up, desolate, and impoverished. But God sees and hears. And he provides. Just as he did for Israel. Just as he did for Moses. He sees you even now. Hear his words: "I have seen, I have heard, and I am concerned about you."

CHAPTER 9

THE HEART
OF THE FATHER

IN THE FALL OF 2008, I enjoyed the luxury of breaking away from the meetings and activity of the church office for several days of study and reflection at a cottage on the Lake Michigan shoreline. On Thursday afternoon that week I drove to an area Chinese restaurant to have a late lunch and to get some reading done. The following January I would be preaching a series of sermons from Proverbs on personal finances. In addition to scouring the Proverbs for pertinent instruction related to working, saving, spending, and borrowing, I also dove into a couple books on personal money management. So I was cradling a family budgeting book in one hand and my chopsticks in the other.

My booth faced the wall of the restaurant where a flat-screen TV played a CNN continuous-news program. The volume was turned down, but bold captions and creative graphics reported the news. If you watch TV news, you know that there can be a lot going on at once. An attractive anchor talks while subtitles relay his or her words. Another box appears to the right of the anchor presenting the charts and graphs pertinent to the story. At the bottom of the screen a thin ribbon scrolls, detailing breaking news bits that may be totally unrelated to the story the anchor is presenting. Then there is the small box in the lower right-hand corner relating second-by-second changes in the financial markets — the Dow Jones Industrial Average, S&P 500, and Nasdaq. A lot is going on at once.

As I sat nibbling at my food, casually reading the budgeting book, highlighting insightful illustrations and recommendations for personal finances that might be helpful in the sermon series, the silent TV gave steady, depressing financial news. It was Thursday, October 9, the one-year anniversary of the all-time high of the Dow Jones Industrial Average (14,164). A headline read: "Dow drops below 9000 for the first time since 2003." A supplemental box appeared in the corner of the screen, depicting the Dow dropping by the second. Dropping, dropping, dropping.

"Dow down 38% in one year," the new caption read. As I ate and read and watched, I wondered how these declining numbers would affect me. For ten years I had been squirreling away money in a retirement account. Month after month I faithfully set aside funds to be deposited, and hopefully grow, toward some distant day out in the future when I would no longer be able to work. And as I was watching the news I was doing some math. *Down 38 percent in one year,* I thought to myself. *If my funds have dropped as much as the Dow dropped, then I only have about 60 percent of what I had a year ago.* I am in my midforties and nowhere near retirement, but I wondered how this would affect me someday. My thoughts moved to my friends who were in their midsixties and how this might affect their lives, decisions, and lifestyles.

The day I was sitting in the Chinese buffet, the Dow lost 678 points — 7 percent of its value in a single day. And this was the seventh day in a row it had dropped, 17 percent so far that week. It would dip again the next day. I had a sense that the stakes had just gone up for the sermon series I was preparing.

Four days later, a General Motors plant across town announced that it would be closing its doors. The plant closing was just one in a series of slowdowns, shutdowns, downscaling moves, and downsizing initiatives indicative of the manufacturing climate in our area. And Grand Rapids remains healthier than many of the hardest hit cities in the Great Lakes region.

The Ripple Effect

What these numbers on the TV meant in human toll was that many in their late fifties with retirement plans would be recalculating, wondering if they would be working into their late sixties. It also meant that many of them would not have the option of when to retire. Many would be "encouraged" to take early retirement so that their companies could hire younger, cheaper labor — workers in their early thirties who do not carry the liability of decades of accumulated raises and several weeks of vacation a year. High school and college graduates alike would face a radically different prospect upon graduation than older siblings who entered the workforce only five years earlier.

The numbers on the screen meant that record home foreclosures would continue. As foreclosed houses flood the market, home prices plummet due to the number of bargains available. For many, the selling price of their home now falls well below the amount of their mortgage. It is common to encounter families in a situation in which they need to relocate to a better job market but cannot sell a house in order to move. This prospect routinely presents an "I can't afford to stay yet I can't afford to move" scenario.

Though a discussion about how God may be at work redemptively through the Land Between is a timeless conversation, the current economic crisis pushes this topic into increased relevance for many of us. The loss of manufacturing jobs, the high rates of unemployment, a volatile stock market, and the collapse of the housing market accompanied by record foreclosures and personal bankruptcy mean that more of us will find ourselves in difficult and unwanted transitions. Though timeless, this Land Between conversation is timely.

"Is the Lord's Arm Too Short?"

God is prepared to multiply leaders to help Moses carry the weight of leading the Israelites, but the meat issue is still a considerable problem to resolve. Moses is still at a loss concerning how to face the raging crisis about manna and the demand for meat. In the wilderness, a place of barren waste, how can Moses respond to the demand for food? God will provide here also.

In what seems to Moses an absurd promise, the Lord announces that he has heard the people's complaint and will provide meat. Not simply a sandwich or two, not meat for a meal or a day, but enough for an entire month. Moses reacts with stunned disbelief. He protests: "Here I am among six hundred thousand men on foot, and you say, 'I will give them meat to eat for a whole month!' Would they have enough if flocks and herds were slaughtered for them? Would they have enough if all the fish in the sea were caught for them?" (Numbers 11:21–22).

Moses can't imagine how such a need could possibly be met. Here they are in the wilderness! If every goat was barbecued and every lamb roasted, there wouldn't be food for a month. Moses couldn't imagine a supply of food this abundant if the sea were emptied of its fish. God responds to Moses' disbelief with a challenging question: "Is the LORD's arm too short?" (v. 23). Moses, are you questioning my ability? Is my capacity in doubt?

God's response to Moses here is a powerful reminder for us when we come to the end of our resources, become anxious, and begin to doubt God's provision. In your Land Between circumstances, listen for this question: "Is the Lord's arm too short?"

Do Not Worry

As we reflect on God's ability to meet our needs, let's go back to Jesus' teaching on the lilies of the field. Remember what he said? "If that is how God clothes the grass of the field, which is here today and tomorrow is thrown into the fire, will he not much more clothe you, O you of little faith?" (Matthew 6:30). It will be helpful here to consider some context for this teaching so we can understand how important it is to God that we live free of the anxiety that threatens to consume us in the Land Between.

Central to Jesus' mission was to reveal the heart of God the Father. He told his disciples, "Anyone who has seen me has seen the Father" (John 14:9). In essence, Jesus was saying, "Spend time with me, listen to me, watch me, and you will see what is in the heart of God."

When the disciples request of Jesus, "Teach us to pray," he responds with words that are commonly referred to as the Lord's Prayer (Luke 11). Embedded in this model prayer is the supplication: "Give us each day our daily bread" (v. 3). This is how Jesus taught his followers to approach their Father in heaven. "Father, please provide the things I need today." It is a daily prayer for our daily needs, resting in the certainty that God provides. God wants us to trust him this way — for every need.

People flocked to Jesus as his popularity grew. Seeing the crowds one day, he called his disciples, sat down, and began teaching. The material that followed is commonly called the Sermon on the Mount and is found in Matthew 6 – 8. Among other foundational teachings in this section of Scripture is Jesus' directive against being consumed by anxiety. When Jesus addressed this issue, his instruction was anchored in the assumption that God the Father sees, cares, and provides. Jesus instructed his followers, "Do not worry about your life, what you will eat or drink; or about your body, what you will wear" (6:25).

The nature of his warning tells us something of the economic climate of Jesus' day and the poverty endured by many of those listening. Jesus challenged his followers not to become anxious about securing the basic needs of life such as food and clothing. Concerning anxiety over food, Jesus drew his disciples' attention to the birds: "Look at the birds of the air; they do not sow or reap or store away in barns, and yet your heavenly Father feeds them. Are you not much more valuable than they?" (6:26).

Since this teaching took place in an outdoor setting, it is reasonable to imagine that birds were visible as Jesus spoke. Did he gesture to a flock as he taught? He challenged his disciples to consider that the birds do not plant crops, harvest, or store away stashes of food the way people do. Instead, God provides them with what they need. Jesus then asked, "Are you not much more valuable than they [the birds]?" (6:26). His line of reasoning was that if the Creator cares for the birds, he will care passionately about providing for his children.

Then Jesus drove home his point: "So do not worry, saying, 'What shall we eat?' or 'What shall we drink?' or 'What shall we wear?' For the pagans run after all these things, and your heavenly Father knows that you need them" (6:31–32). He is saying, "Don't worry. Don't give in to anxiety. Don't let it take your energy. Don't let it control you. Trust God. He sees. He knows."

When Jesus speaks of the "pagans running after all these things," I think he means that consuming anxiety is the expected response of those who have no connection to the true and living God. We live a life of troubled anxiety when we forget that God is the God who sees, the God who knows, the God who cares. Our Father loves to provide. Providing is what he does. He sees our most intimate needs. He knows our hearts. Knows our suffering. Knows every detail about our journey in the Land Between. Hear Jesus' words: "Do not worry ... your heavenly Father knows."

"The Lord Will Provide"

Now let's go back to Abraham to consider someone who believed in Jesus' encouragement to trust God well before Jesus came to earth. We have already reviewed the facts of the story.

At last a child is born to Abraham and Sarah. His name is Isaac, which means "laughter." It was comedy that a baby would be born to a couple at such an advanced age. A stranger seeing Isaac with his father might suspect they are grandfather and grandson rather than father and cherished son.

Abraham ages and Isaac matures. As Abraham sees the child of promise interacting with servants or leading sheep out to pasture, he knows that he is looking at the future. The blessing for which Abraham traveled and waited will be transmitted from father to son. The great nation through which the world will be blessed will now come through Abraham's son, "Laughter."

It is at this time that Abraham has one final upsetting adventure in faith. "Some time later God tested Abraham.... God said, 'Take your son, your only son, Isaac, whom you love.... Sacrifice him ... as a burnt offering on one of the mountains I will tell you about'" (Genesis 22:1–2).

We are told that God is testing Abraham. It is as if the events that unfold are so disturbing the reader needs to be urged at the beginning not to worry. "Nothing's going to happen to the kid. He will come back alive. God is just testing

Abraham." This is information that the reader now possesses, but as the story unfolds, we need to remember that Abraham does not have this information. He only knows that God has said, "Take your son and sacrifice him."

The wording is similar to the initial call upon Abraham's life. In the beginning of Abraham's narrative, he is told to go to a land that God will show him. Now, in this severe test, Abraham is told to go to a mountain that God will show him. Both commands required a journey into the unknown. "Abraham, years ago you trusted me by letting go of your past. Now will you trust me by letting go of your future?"

The story unfolds in slow motion with revealing detail. Abraham rises early in the morning and places a saddle on a donkey. He chops firewood for the offering and brings two servants on the journey to the mountain appointed by God. At the top, Abraham builds an altar and places the wood on it. He then ties up Isaac and lays him on the wood, preparing to sacrifice his son. In God's perfect timing, not a second too late, the angel of the Lord calls out, "Do not lay a hand on the boy. Do not do anything to him. Now I know that you fear God, because you have not withheld from me your son, your only son" (Genesis 22:12).

Just then Abraham sees a ram nearby, so he sacrifices the ram instead of his son. The son lives. The ram dies. Abraham passes this agonizing trial of faith. He names the mountain "The LORD Will Provide" (Genesis 22:14). From beginning to end, God has provided for Abraham, and throughout his journey, the question has remained the same: "Will you trust me completely?" Abraham's obedience in this final test resounds as a yes. "Yes, I have trusted you with my past, and, yes, I will trust you with my future."

The Chance to Trust

Once again, the Israelites in the desert were in full possession of these details. They knew that Abraham had embarked on a journey of trust in which God had shown himself faithful. But though they were familiar with Abraham's life of faith, they seemed to have learned little from these stories. This loss of spiritual legacy is deeply troubling, for while they were physical descendants of Abraham, they seem to have let go of the privilege and responsibility of being his spiritual descendants.

I don't think the Israelites forgot Abraham's story but, rather, did not apply it. They failed to comprehend how Abraham's journey affected theirs. They had known of God's faithfulness in theory, but now they would be called upon to know through experience. In the desert, "theoretical knowledge" was to become "experiential knowledge." They "knew" from the Abraham story that God was the God who provides, but now they would have the chance to learn for themselves.

This was the Israelites' chance to learn trust, to risk trust, to become a people of trust. Again and again they would miss

PART 4

DISCIPLINE

CHAPTER 10

THE DISCIPLINARIAN

RONNIE IS A TENTH-GRADE BASKETBALL PLAYER full of potential. After basketball practice one afternoon, his coach asked to see him in his office. Ronnie was leading the junior varsity team in scoring and rebounding. He measured six feet, six inches and was still growing. Rapid growth is often accompanied by gangly awkwardness, but his height was matched by uncommon agility and coordination. Partway through the season, the coaching staff even considered moving him up to the varsity team. Rarely had they seen such promise in a maturing young player. Basketball seemed to come so naturally that Ronnie was a dominant force without even working at it. And that was the problem — the reason he was in the coach's office. He wasn't working at it.

Discipline issues with Ronnie were becoming an increasing concern. He was routinely showing up for practice fifteen minutes late with no explanation. During practice he behaved as if immune to correction, sometimes even rolling his eyes at a coach's directives. It was as if his high level of performance exempted him from the need to be coached. The previous day he had skipped a mandatory team meeting because he "forgot."

Ronnie walked through the locker room, swung open the door to the coach's office without knocking, and was surprised to see the varsity coach present as well.

"Ronnie, have a seat," his coach said, motioning to the empty chair in the room.

"You are an outstanding player with incredible potential," his coach began. "But your unwillingness to receive correction, your refusal to arrive at practice on time, and your contempt for the coaching staff are poisoning this team." The coach's words were firm and measured. "I have decided that you will be benched for the next two games. You will dress and warm up, but you will not play — even if we are behind."

The conviction with which the brief speech was delivered left the impression that this decision was not going to be negotiated.

The varsity coach had been silent until this point. "Ronnie," he added, "I fully agree with Coach Jackson's decision. I've been watching you since you were in the seventh grade, and I believe you're one of the strongest players ever to come through these doors. Your talent is without question. But you need to hear something loud and clear: either your attitude changes or you will not be playing basketball for me next season. I will not allow disrespect on my team. Am I clear?"

In being benched, Ronnie may feel as if the coach is trying to destroy his season, but a mature observer will recognize that the coach is disciplining Ronnie in an attempt to rescue his season, and possibly his future in team sports. That is what good discipline does. It inflicts pain in order to save or rescue something. I have to wonder, when God disciplines us in ways that seem harsh or difficult to bear, could it be that he is attempting to rescue something?

A Harsh Disciplinarian

Revisiting the Israelites as they demand meat in the desert, we are about to see God provide for them but not exactly in the way we expect. The meat is not going to arrive as a tenderly bestowed meal. In giving them what they want, God is about to take the posture of a harsh disciplinarian. Just listen to how Moses extends God's promise of provision: "The LORD heard you when you wailed, 'If only we had meat to eat! We were better off in Egypt!' Now the LORD will give you meat, and you will eat it. You will not eat it for just one day, or two days, or five, ten or twenty days, but for a whole month—until it comes out of your nostrils and you loathe it" (Numbers 11:18–20).

With the provision of meat comes the disciplining hand of God. As uncomfortable as this part of the story is, we must try to understand it to learn from it. The Land Between is fertile ground for God's discipline.

God responds to his people's demand for food by sending the mother of all quail migrations their way. There was a history of quail migrating from Europe and West Asia to Africa in enormous numbers. "Now a wind went out from the LORD and drove quail in from the sea. It brought them down all around the camp to about three feet above the ground, as far as a day's walk in any direction. All that day and night and all the next day the people went out and gathered quail. No one gathered less than ten homers. Then they spread them out all around the camp" (Numbers 11:31–32).

A homer is estimated to be somewhere between four and six bushels. When a person collected ten homers of quail, this would amount to roughly forty to sixty bushels—in other words, a truckload. The mention of spreading the meat out around the camp probably refers to drying the meat so it could be preserved.

The loathsome manna diet is now supplemented by amounts of meat that defy the imagination. The people have what they want, and the crisis is over. Well . . . not quite yet. Watch what happens: "But while the meat was still between their teeth and before it could be consumed, the anger of the LORD burned against the people, and he struck them with a severe plague. Therefore the place was named Kibroth Hattaavah, because there they buried the people who had craved other food" (Numbers 11:33 – 34).

Did you see that? People died. The quail arrived, and so did a plague. That is harsh discipline.

The Land Between is painful terrain to traverse. Often we make it more painful than it needs to be. Our actions, reactions, and overreactions can compound the situation. The journey through the desert was difficult for the Israelites, but they exacerbated their own pain. They locked into a pattern of complaining and demanding, a pattern of ingratitude and distrust. They ended up getting the meat they wanted, but when the quail arrived, it was a spoiled meal.

On the most basic level, I believe this still happens. We enter the Land Between, a difficult space, but our obstinacy can make the situation more difficult than it needs to be. There may be times when we get the meal we demand, but we may also find it spoiled when it arrives.

The Consequences of Our Demands

The Johnsons grow increasingly ungrateful about their home. So many of their friends are "moving up," but they have to stay in the same house year after year. They feel as if they're driving in the financial slow lane, watching everybody else fly by. And they are tired of waiting. First, they do a little bit of plotting and stretching, then some scheming and more stretching, until, finally, they move into the house of their dreams — with a staggering mortgage taking them close to the edge of what their income can cover.

Then there are those expenses to which the Johnsons willingly turn a blind eye — higher taxes, increased insurance, and more furnishings. Just to provide basic furniture for each room pushes them so close to the edge of a financial precipice that they can see the yawning ravine of disaster feet away. Then comes word that Mr. Johnson's hours at work have been reduced and that the "guaranteed bonus" isn't coming through this year. Mrs. Johnson's work is cut from full-time to part-time. They tumble over the edge. A second missed payment, a late notice on a credit card — the house of their dreams has become a financial nightmare.

"Why did we have to have this place?" they ask, sitting in the half-furnished dining room, arguing over which bills to pay and which to delay.

They got the meal they demanded, but it was a spoiled meal.

.....

Kate is weary of being alone. How many bridesmaid's dresses will she buy before trying on a wedding dress of her own? What slows her movement toward marriage is that she has been limiting her options. Since high school she has only been willing to date men who demonstrate strong Christian character. This decision drastically limits the field of options. Now her longing becomes a demand. She gives God an ultimatum: "Okay, God, here's the deal. I would prefer a man with a spiritual pulse. And you have three months to deliver. After that, I'm going shopping for a guy regardless of spiritual temperature or heart for things eternal."

Three months come and go.

In stubbornness and distrust, she takes matters into her own hands and steers a course toward headache and heartache. There is a strong likelihood that Kate will get the meal she demands, but when it arrives, it may come as a spoiled meal.

.....

The Land Between is difficult terrain. We make it exceedingly more difficult when our patience dwindles and we demand that God respond in our timing and on our terms.

But why did people have to die in the desert? God sends a plague and people die. Doesn't this seem a little over the top? If a basketball coach has an insolent, disrespectful player, he benches him — he doesn't kill him. Isn't this a little heavy-handed? Is this severe discipline in the desert really necessary?

"There they buried the people who had craved other food." The plague with which the Lord "struck them" is fatal to some. Is there anything about this picture that sits uncomfortably with our image of a loving, caring, helpful God? Does it seem a bit, well, un-Jesus-y to you? I remember this Bible story from childhood, but not the judgment part. The part I remember is "God is good and feeds the people manna and quail," not "God gets angry while feeding the people manna and quail, and he kills some of them for complaining." What's going on here?

Sometimes God will give us what we demand and let us take the consequences. This is not because he hates us or has given up on us. As harsh as those consequences may be, they are still under the control of a God who loves us and a God who sees. He sees the big picture. He sees what's coming. He knows the events and challenges for which we need to be prepared. In Hebrews, we read, "No discipline seems pleasant at the time, but painful. Later on, however, it produces a harvest of righteousness and peace for those who have been trained by it" (12:11).

God's discipline trains us. It produces righteousness and peace. And God knows we desperately need these things. Just as a caring coach disciplines a player, God, in his care, may send a corrective discipline into the lives of his children. His discipline is intended to prepare us for the challenges and conflicts that lie in our future.

CHAPTER 11

LEARNING
FROM MISTAKES

MAYBE YOU HAVE NOTICED THOSE POSTERS hanging in offices. A photograph of a transcendently beautiful nature scene or a stunning athletic image. Perhaps a soaring eagle or a pole vaulter just clearing the bar. Below the photograph is a single word caption: PERSISTENCE, TEAMWORK, or VISION printed in a large enough font to be read from across the room. Then there is the smaller motivational quote at the bottom, extolling a particular virtue. These images, captions, and quotes are intended to inspire and motivate positive activity.

The items available at despair.com offer a humorous parody of these motivational posters. The website's lithographs also portray stunning photography and large-font single-word captions, but the quotes at the bottom are humorously de-motivational. An enormous grizzly bear stands in a rushing river, mouth open, about to devour a fish that has dutifully migrated upstream. The caption: AMBITION. The quote: "The journey of a thousand miles sometimes ends very, very badly."

One image shows the silhouette of a lone backpacker at the base of an ominous mountain, preparing for a courageous climb. The caption: CHALLENGES. The quote: "I expected times like this, but I never thought they'd be so bad, so long, and so frequent."

Another poster depicts an ocean scene with the bow of a lone sunken ship protruding from the water. The caption: MISTAKES. The quote: "It could be that the purpose of your life is only to serve as a warning to others." This poster is particularly appropriate as we consider the desert wanderings of the Israelites. Many events from the Israelites' wilderness experience seem to serve as warnings to the reader: "Don't do this!" Much of the impact we glean from the narrative hinges on wildly negative example. As we explore the Israelites' rebellion over manna and demand for meat, we engage a story where God's people are clearly not at their best. The events recorded for us in the desert provide a cautionary tale of what not to become. In other words, as we journey through the Land Between, we have the privilege of learning from the Israelites' mistakes. We witness a shipwreck and, in so doing, gain insight about how to avoid our own. On the bow of the broken ship, a sign reads, "Treacherous Shoreline." The message is clear: "Don't end up like us."

Equipped for Every Good Work

Listen in on a conversation between one of the most important leaders in the early Jesus movement and a younger pastor he has trained. These words were written by Paul to Timothy shortly before Paul's execution in Rome. Paul reminds the younger pastor: "All Scripture is God-breathed and is useful for teaching, rebuking, correcting and training in righteousness, so that the man of God may be thoroughly equipped for every good work" (2 Timothy 3:16–17).

When Paul wrote these words, The New Testament of the Bible had not yet been compiled, so when Paul spoke of "Scripture," he was referring to the Jewish Scriptures, or what is commonly referred to as the Old Testament. Paul is reminding Timothy of the usefulness of the Old Testament Scriptures, among which we find our story about the Israelites, manna, and complaint. These stories are intended to "thoroughly" equip the people of God for lives of goodness ("for every good work"). Of the terms Paul used to describe the usefulness of Scripture, note especially that it is useful for "rebuking" and "correcting." These terms indicate a desperately needed change of direction.

If I am traveling toward hazardous waters, stories from the Bible can serve as warning signs. "Shallow Reef," they warn in bold letters. This is powerfully good news. If the Scriptures are replete with cautionary tales, then as I read my Bible or listen to the Scriptures taught, I can correct my course by seeing what happened to others. I can avoid severe discipline by amending my way via instruction rather than having to experience the wounds of severe discipline myself. We don't have to travel the route of repeated error. We get to watch people like the Israelites travel it and make the needed adjustments.

This is a lifesaving wonder. Let me repeat: instead of learning just from our own mistakes, we who have the privilege of holding a Bible in our hands can also learn from the mistakes of people in the Bible narratives. Not only can we learn from self-inflicted wounds in our lives, but we can also learn from needless pain in *their* lives.

Paul encouraged some early Jesus followers specifically about looking to the Israelites' example in this way. In another one of his letters, Paul refers to the Israelites' rebellions in the desert and pleads with the Jesus followers living in the Greek city of Corinth to learn from the severe mistakes that were made in the wilderness. Paul counsels: "These things happened to them as examples and were written down as warnings for us, on whom the fulfillment of the ages has come. So, if you think you are standing firm, be careful that you don't fall! No temptation has seized you except what is common to man. And God is faithful; he will not let you be tempted beyond what you can bear. But when you are tempted, he will also provide a way out so that you can stand up under it" (1 Corinthians 10:11–13).

Once again, the stories in the Scriptures should serve as examples. They were recorded as warnings for us. If we think we are immune, we should think again (lest we fall). The story of the desert is a story for us to absorb through our pores, roll over in our minds, and meditate on. Note especially the words toward the end of Paul's warning to the Corinthian Christians. He reminds them that "God is faithful." God will provide for you when you are stretched, pulled, and tested. This is a comfort when we travel through the Land Between. The Scriptures tell us God will be faithful. He will provide what we need each day. Through the confusion, pain, and dying dreams, our Father in heaven desires to guide us at every turn.

The Nature of the Offense

To fully explore the story of the Israelites in the desert, we must further address the issue of God's discipline. As we dig deeper into the narrative, I hope we will grow in our appreciation of what God is attempting to accomplish through the severe punishment he inflicts in the wilderness. Discipline is the activity of inflicting pain for redemptive purposes, and it is something for which God is to be admired, appreciated, and esteemed. Remember the words from the book of Hebrews, which we read in chapter 10: discipline produces righteousness and peace.

Let's spend some time together exploring more deeply the nature of the Israelites' offense and the history of the offenders. We looked into these subjects earlier, but to get a better understanding of God's actions in the desert, we will need to revisit them here.

First, let's look again at the nature of the offense. On first glance, it seems as if the Israelites simply grew weary of manna and complained about their lack of meat. God's response, however, reveals the heart of the people's crime and gives us more insight into why God's judgment was so severe. "The LORD heard you when you wailed, 'If only we had meat to eat! We were better off in Egypt!' Now the LORD will give you meat, and you will eat it. You will not eat it for just one day, or two days, or five, ten or twenty days, but for a whole month — until it comes out of your nostrils and you loathe it — because you have rejected the LORD, who is among you, and have wailed before him, saying, 'Why did we ever leave Egypt?' " (Numbers 11:18 – 20).

Here we find the full force of the people's crime. Notice the two references to Egypt in this brief passage. As the Lord unleashes his rebuke, he repeats the people's complaint: "We were better off in Egypt!" and then a few lines later, "[you] have wailed before him, saying, 'Why did we ever leave Egypt.' " This is a crime that is far more serious than mere complaining about cafeteria food. What they wail is a serious accusation against God. In claiming that they were better off in Egypt, they are basically screaming, "God, we were better off without you!"

This gives weight to the indictment, "You have rejected the LORD, who is among you." In fact, the Lord's presence was literally "among" them. Moses was not speaking figuratively. The wilderness camp of the Israelites was set up in a configuration where the twelve tribes surrounded the center of the camp—three tribes each to the north, south, east, and west. In the middle of the configured tents was the tabernacle, or Tent of Meeting. This portable worship center housed the ark of the covenant in an inner room called the Holy of Holies. This was the holiest space of holy spaces, and it was the portal to the presence of God. Understand the accusation, "You have rejected the LORD, who is among you": literally, God's presence had come to deliver and to dwell "among" the people— right there in the middle of the camp.

Understanding what was in the heart of the Israelites is critical as we discuss God's discipline here. As God's judgment falls on the people, we must be clear about what the offense is. To repeat, the crime went deeper than griping about their manna diet; the crime was treason. "We were better off without you as our rescuer, we were better off without your presence, we were better off as slaves, we would have had a better life living among the gods of Egypt." This is serious.

The History of the Offenders

In addition to examining the severe nature of their offense, let's recall the Israelites' history in the desert up to this point.

The Israelites' complaint about food and then God's harsh discipline do not suddenly materialize out of thin air but occur within a moving story. As we have already discussed, these people had a history of complaint. The grievance over food is not an isolated, uncharacteristic moment of murmuring but one in a series of gripe fests to which the people have fallen prey ever since they departed Egypt two years earlier.

The sons and daughters of Jacob have an established pattern of grumbling against God. Let's review a partial list of infractions. At the Red Sea crossing, fearing for their lives, the people yell at Moses, "What have you done to us by bringing us out of Egypt? Didn't we say to you in Egypt, 'Leave us alone; let us serve the Egyptians'?" (Exodus 14:11 – 12). Later, consumed with thirst, they again wail against Moses when they arrive at a source of water only to find it undrinkable. After this, driven by hunger, they groan at Moses, despairing over their lack of food. Then another water crisis arises, and true to form, they respond with rancor toward their leader. Do you feel like a judge thumbing through a thick "rap sheet" of an accused person? The Israelites are repeat offenders, which I believe is key.

As we review this history of complaint, let's remember what God was working to accomplish. Trust is the glue that holds any relationship together. Throughout these hardships, God desired to forge a people of trust. "I need you to trust me," he seems to be saying again and again as he meets each of the Israelites' hardships with his provision. Remember, the Israelites are the people of promise, headed for the Land of Promise, and they are totally unfit to take possession of the land in their current condition. They really don't know God or trust him. The purpose of the desert is to forge a relationship of trust.

For people who refuse to learn, we use terms like "unteachable" or "incorrigible." King Solomon, son of David, added this memorable wisdom bite to his collection of proverbs: "As a dog returns to its vomit, so a fool repeats his folly" (Proverbs 26:11). This memorably disgusting pearl of wisdom seeks to describe the propensity of those lacking in discretion to return to the same mistakes again and again.

Let's turn the spotlight away from the desert wanderers and toward ourselves. Like the chronic complainers in the wilderness, the tragedy is not that we make mistakes but that we are prone to make the same mistakes. The heartache is not that we experience pain but that so much of our pain goes wasted when we refuse to learn from it.

Repeat Offenders

In an honest and vulnerable moment, a friend reveals the financial pressure her family is facing. They owe more on their vehicles than the cars are worth, they are upside down on their mortgage, and the high interest of credit card debt is killing them. You listen sympathetically. Two weeks later you learn of an elaborate vacation the family is planning, a trip that will add to the compounding money struggles they are experiencing. *How much pain do people need to experience before they change?* you wonder.

.....

The first offense was that of a minor in possession of alcohol and resulted in a required sequence of weekend classes. The court intended these classes to be inconvenient enough to act as a deterrent, but the classes did nothing to alter his habits. The second offense led to community service and more classes. Then came the DUI and a restricted driver's license. His car insurance rates rocketed. And yet the behavior remained unchanged, even as the cost got ever higher. The pain was going wasted.

.....

In the Israelites' desert story, the great tragedy is that the pain seems to go wasted. Warnings go unheeded, and because of this, a whole generation is in jeopardy of missing out on the promised blessing. If this continues, they will doom themselves. How often do we do the same in our own lives? Lord, have mercy on us. In fact, this is what God does. As we will see, his discipline *is* his mercy.

When we study the biblical account in context, we understand that the manna revolt and the discipline do not occur at the beginning of the Israelites' journey. They have been rescued from a pursuing army at the Red Sea and rescued from their thirst and hunger with God's provision in the desert. At Mount Sinai they received the commandments outlining their covenant with God, and later they constructed the tabernacle for the presence of God in the middle of their camp. They are now nearing the gateway to the land promised to their forefathers. They are no longer at the beginning of their journey, yet they are still behaving like beginners. They seem no closer to actually trusting their God than at the beginning of the wilderness experience. Their repeated refrain remains, "We don't trust you."

This is a critical point. The Israelites do not seem to have changed over the course of two years in the wilderness. In reading their story, I have the sensation of listening to an old-fashioned record player with the needle stuck in a groove, repeating the same fragment of song again and again. Here the dissonant tune repeats itself over and over: "Hardship intended to build trust results instead in contemptuous complaint." The harsh discipline of the quail plague is not severity for its own sake — it is intended to dislodge the Israelites from the rut of their lethal, faith-destroying groove. As is true in our lives, here with the Israelites, God is at work to rescue.

CHAPTER 12

REDEMPTIVE PAIN

AFTER GRADUATING FROM HIGH SCHOOL, MY youngest child, Alex, moved to Ukraine to assist a small church. What started out as a three-month trip has now extended to two years. Despite the distance, I think we have more face-to-face communication with him on the other side of the world than when he is home and our lives often orbit past each other without connection. Every week we chat virtually, Alex looking into his web cam and I into mine. He called to chat last week, days after his twentieth birthday. He had just come off a hard week, having faced some truly stressful challenges.

The pastor of the church where he serves asked Alex to preach last weekend. This was only Alex's third sermon, so he is new to the time-intensive process of preparation. He has taken leadership of the music ministry in the small congregation, and the day before he preached, he was responsible for a worship event. Adding tension to his heavy week was a conflict with his landlord, who is demanding that he pay back utilities. This was not part of their agreement when Alex moved into his flat months ago, and the conflict remains unresolved. Also, a close Ukrainian friend has experienced some significant medical issues, adding to the strain.

Though it was a difficult week for Alex, I am grateful he had to endure it. I believe God is molding him into a leader, and this molding will require pressure as part of his formation. I am thankful for the trials my son experiences and for the hardships he faces. It is my belief that he is not only maturing as a man but also as a man of God. I trust that God will use the difficulties and challenges in Alex's life to transform him. Far from being alarmed by my son's burdens, I give thanks, because I know that he is being stretched and pulled for a reason. Alex is being provided with an opportunity to become a man of faith, a man of trust.

When I asked how he was able to prepare and preach with everything else going on at that time, he responded, "I felt like God carried me through the week." I am deeply moved by these words and am grateful that he is responding to struggle in a way that draws him near to God. I suspect that he is being prepared for far greater challenges in the future and that these early lessons are critical to his growth.

.....

At 5:15 in the morning, cars begin to pull into the parking lot.

Later in the day, the temperatures will rise to the midtwenties, but as men and women exit their vehicles and enter the gym, it is a brisk 14 degrees. They have answered the call of their alarm clocks and driven through the cold to spend an hour with a fitness instructor, who will stand in front of the group and lead them through a series of exercises that will challenge, push, and stretch them. Here is the crazy part: they pay money for this. They pay for someone to inflict pain on them, because they believe this pain is purposeful.

A mother of preschoolers makes this pilgrimage three times a week in an attempt to recover the figure she had before a succession of pregnancies. A thirty-two-year-old man shows up religiously, motivated to get back in shape after a casual touch football game over the holidays left him gasping for breath. A couple registered for their first triathlon hope to improve their core fitness level. And a future bride hopes to fit into a smaller-sized dress when the spring wedding arrives. Though they may not use this terminology, each person understands the concept that pain can be purposeful. They comprehend this or they wouldn't rise from their beds, drive through the snow, and pay someone to hurt them.

This picture of the early morning gym can be helpful in understanding redemptive pain. It reminds us that pain is something we willingly embrace when we believe it will serve a helpful purpose. Our perspective on the harsh discipline of the desert will gain clarity and significance if we recognize that God's use of pain is redemptive. He is at work to rescue something.

What Is at Stake

We left the Israelites stricken by plague in the desert, having buried some of their own. To fully appreciate what is at stake for them—and why God might have afflicted them so severely—let's turn our attention to a critical, pivotal event that occurs shortly *after* "the manna riots" of Numbers 11. One of the most tragic incidents in the whole exodus story occurs just two chapters later.

In Numbers 13, only a couple pages after the manna and quail disaster, the Israelites are camped at a place called Kadesh Barnea. From here Moses sends a dozen spies into Canaan, the Promised Land, in preparation for an invasion. Timing here is critical. It seems that the complaining and demanding about not having meat to eat occurred on the doorstep of the Land of Promise. At the time of the quail ordeal, the Israelites are close—very close—to entering the land promised to their forefathers. This would be the climactic moment to which hundreds of years of history had pointed. The promises made to Abraham and confirmed to Isaac and Jacob are about to be fulfilled. Tragically, the people are not ready.

Moses sends twelve spies (one representing each of the tribes) into the land to do some reconnaissance. The spies' mission is to report on the agriculture of the land as well as on its fortifications and the inhabitants' military preparedness. After forty days, the spies return with news that the land is fruitful beyond imagination. They bring back pomegranates, figs, and an enormous cluster of grapes as witness to the fertility of their future home. This is a good land, just as God promised.

But ten of the twelve spies also return with a grim report: The land is good, but sadly, taking it will be impossible. The Israelites would never win a war against such strong inhabitants. "The people who live there are powerful, and the cities are fortified and very large. We even saw descendants of Anak there" (Numbers 13:28). Apparently the Anakites were enormous, dwarfing the Israelites. The spies felt like puny insects by comparison. "We seemed like grasshoppers in our own eyes, and we looked the same to them" (v. 33).

While ten spies poisoned the minds of the people with their version of the mission, the two others — Joshua and Caleb — attempted to sway the people toward trust. "We can do it. God is with us. He will lead us and give the land to us. Do not be afraid." Tragically, the naysayers' majority report swept through the camp and prevailed.

That night the sound of weeping is heard throughout the camp as the Israelites despair over their troubling situation. Then the grumbling begins against Moses and his brother, Aaron: If only they had died in Egypt or in the desert — anything but falling in battle and having their wives and children seized as plunder. Why was God leading them into the land only to be destroyed? In their disillusioned rage, they decide they should select a new leader and return to Egypt. Things are bad, very bad.

In fact, this is one of the darkest moments of the entire exodus travelogue. The consequences of the Israelites' rejection of God here were grievous. The people would not go into the land. They would wander in the desert for forty years — a year for every day the spies were away. In these forty years, the adults who saw the miracles in Egypt, experienced God's provision in the desert, and refused to grow in trust would die in the wilderness. With this final rebellion, the generation prone to chronic complaint and contempt would spend the rest of their days outside the Land of Promise. The joy of the land and the fulfillment of its promises would be transferred to their children. The next generation would go in, but the rebellious, contemptuous, complaining generation would fall in the desert.

This, I believe, was the disaster God was attempting to avert two chapters earlier when he sent a wasting, lethal plague during the quail ordeal. The punishment that accompanied the manna revolt was a shot over the bow, a powerful warning that things would have to be amended immediately if disaster was to be averted. If the Israelites could learn from the plague discipline, then only some of them would have to die in the desert. God intended his discipline to be corrective. He was willing to inflict great pain to prevent astronomical pain. The harsh punishment had been intended to rescue the whole operation.

Disciplining Children

God's discipline can be compared to what we find in a parent-child relationship. We might better understand God's work in our lives if we look at the way the concept of discipline is explored elsewhere in the Bible, particularly in reference to the relationship between fathers and sons.

Proverbs 23:13 tells us: "Do not withhold discipline from a child; if you punish him with the rod, he will not die." Many thoughts and emotions may surface when we read this verse. Hitting a kid with a stick sounds like child abuse, so what is it doing in the Bible? Let's try to understand this instruction in its original setting by taking a trip back to the world where this proverb was given as counsel to parents.

The proverbs were written in an agrarian setting. Families received their livelihood from the field and from the flock. Each season presented a life-and-death struggle, and the laziness of family members could have ruinous results. Decide that plowing feels uncomfortable and you miss your opportunity to have bread that year. Decide to sleep in a few mornings when the grain is ripe and you can lose your crop to locusts or hail. Timing in this culture was everything. But the stakes were even higher than the loss of a crop. If you were careless in raising your crops, you might find yourself in the precarious position of borrowing money for necessities. If you fell behind in your payments, you or your children could become indentured servants to pay off the debt. The proverb "the borrower is servant to the lender" was not taken figuratively. If you were unable to repay someone, you could literally become that person's servant. Or your son or daughter would be led away from your home to the lender's estate as compensation for the unpaid debt. Things would get even harder, because the absence of the children would further decrease your family workforce. This was an unforgiving world with heavy consequences.

Now let's consider the force of these related proverbs: "He who gathers crops in summer is a wise son, but he who sleeps during harvest is a disgraceful son" (10:5). "He who works his land will have abundant food, but the one who chases fantasies will have his fill of poverty" (28:19).

Consider, too, that in the world of Proverbs, massive amounts of responsibility were delegated at a very early age. You may be familiar with the story of David being anointed by the prophet Samuel as Israel's next king. After looking over all of David's brothers, Samuel asks if Jesse has any other sons. The father responds by saying that the youngest is away from home, watching the sheep. Young David is thought to have been about thirteen years old when this incident took place — a junior higher guarding a major portion of the family's net worth. Imagine your eighth grader managing 15 percent of your stock portfolio and you get a good glimpse of their reality. Welcome to the world of the Bible. If your family is depending on those sheep for clothing and food, and if your child sleeps on the job or is careless with sick lambs, you have a serious problem to confront. And it is *your* problem.

Because families lived in an intergenerational setting (parents, grandparents, and grandkids living in the same household), you could work diligently all your life then hand the management of the assets over to your sons, and if they were careless or lazy, you might spend your old age in poverty. Your financial status was intimately linked to their work ethic. In modern Western culture where our children often move away and strike out on their own, we give them advice: "If you make stupid decisions, you could be in trouble." In the world of the proverbs, the father understood something different: "If you make stupid decisions, we are all in trouble."

When the writer of Proverbs, the wise King Solomon, recommends the use of a stick as a motivational tool, it is not over inconsequential issues like failing to feed the dog or turn off the TV. The entire family's welfare depended on vigilance. When Solomon included this proverb in his collection of life wisdom, he was writing for an audience that understood laziness could be lethal. Solomon's challenge seems to be that if you are harvesting your crops early one morning and your kid doesn't show up in the field because he decides he would rather sleep in, you had better get back to the house and get him moving, even if you have to use a stick. The bruising of the stick won't kill this child (he will not die), but lethargy will! If he doesn't learn to get moving, he may drive your entire family toward starvation. The father is inflicting pain in order to save something.

"Discipline your son, for in that there is hope; do not be a willing party to his death" (Proverbs 19:18). "Punish him with the rod and save his soul from death" (23:14). Does our trip back to the agrarian culture of Proverbs cast these teachings on discipline in a new light? In the land of the proverbs, the stick was not applied to the slothful son in hatred but in love. You could be saving your son's life. In fact, if the parent refused to discipline a child, it was noted as a form of passive hatred. "He who spares the rod hates his son, but he who loves him is careful to discipline him" (Proverbs 13:24).

In the land of the proverbs, the severe disciplinary activity of the father was intended as a rescue measure. The willingness of the father to inflict temporary pain on his child was a way of preventing colossal pain. This is clearly God's purpose in the desert when he sends severe discipline on the Israelites in the manna-quail story. He disciplines them to save them.

The author of Hebrews in the New Testament takes it further: "Endure hardship as discipline; God is treating you as sons. For what son is not disciplined by his father?" (12:7). Shouldn't there be space in our thinking for a gracious God who reserves the right to dispense discipline as he sees fit? God often uses painful discipline to mold us, shape us, and rescue us. This, too, is part of God's character. He loves us enough to bring us discomfort to rescue us from attitudes, traits, and habits that will derail our growth and his work in our lives.

Our Stakes

I have an acquaintance whose son received a ticket for a minor infraction. It was one of those "fix-it tickets" for which you simply need to correct the problem — the taillight in this case — and have a police officer sign a statement that it has been corrected. This man's son failed to have the ticket signed, ignoring repeated reminders from the courts.

His parents supplied frequent reminders that he needed to take care of the issue — reminders that the son interpreted as unreasonable nagging. His parents understood that if he was pulled over, an unpaid ticket could be a huge issue. Their warnings, however, remained unheeded and resented. On one occasion, when his mom brought up the issue, the son erupted. "You're treating me like a child! Leave me alone and let me handle this." At that point, his parents complied with his request, leaving the situation fully in their son's hands.

A few weeks later, while driving to his girlfriend's house, the son glanced in the rearview mirror to see the flashing lights of a squad car. The officer ran his plates in the computer and discovered there was a bench warrant for the young man's arrest. In front of his girlfriend's house, with her parents watching, he was searched, handcuffed, placed in the squad car, and driven to the small suburban jail. In order to be released, he would need to pay a fine, which had now grown to over $2,000. He called home and humbly asked his dad to come down, pay the fine, and get him out. His dad replied, "I'm so sorry. Your mother and I would love to help you out, but unfortunately, we made a commitment to you that we would not get involved and that we would let you handle this. We need to honor that commitment. You're on your own."

My friend confided in me that after a couple days, when his son would be transferred to a downtown jail, which truly had the potential of being physically dangerous, he was going to step in and get his kid out. But in the meantime, the son was feeling the pain of discipline — not because his father hated him, but because his father loved him. This man knew the stakes if his son failed to correct certain weaknesses of character. The stakes would only get higher with time. This father knew, and he was out to rescue something.

.....

You are standing in the checkout lane. A war is unfolding in the cart in front of you. A three-year-old, overdue for a nap, begins to demand cookies from the cart. Her mom tells her that those are for later, but the preschooler whines, "I want them now." "No, honey," her mom reasons, "we will have one after lunch when we get home." The toddler turns up the volume, no longer requesting but now demanding. She begins to kick her dangling feet against the cart. What you are witnessing is about to become a full-blown hostage situation: "Either my demands are met within seconds," the child is saying in her way, "or there will be an incident."

Heads are beginning to turn, and the mom, trying to avoid a public scene, caves. "Just one," she negotiates. As she opens the box of cookies and indulges the child, something in you silently pleads for the mother to take charge. You want to blurt out, "If you cave like this, your home will be run by a three-year-old!"

These seemingly small moments are exceptionally important tests for us as parents. We tend to forget that we are not raising children — we are raising adults. My job as a dad is much more difficult than simply ensuring I have compliant children. My task is to raise adults who will not act as if they are the center of the universe. Left to themselves, self-centered children have a way of becoming narcissistic employees, husbands, and wives. The goal of discipline is to correct behavior early while the stakes are low — as with a tantrum in the checkout lane. But stakes keep rising as a child grows, dates, marries, and produces offspring. A life marked by self-centeredness can result in a nasty toll as a person's sphere of influence expands.

Let's put the spotlight back on ourselves. As God's children, we are subject to his discipline for the same reasons. The further we get on the journey of life, the higher the stakes become. Only God knows our future, and he wants us to be equipped for what lies ahead. He wants us to grow into the people he intends us to be, not controlled by character deficits but having the strengths of a Christlike character. In the Land Between, God is very interested in the people we are becoming. He is willing to use corrective discipline to mold, shape, and refine us.

PART 5

GROWTH

CHAPTER 13

THE DESERT CROP

EACH JULY, TRAVERSE CITY, MICHIGAN, HOSTS the National Cherry Festival. The freshwater bays of Lake Michigan flanking the city make it a desired vacation spot, but agriculture has been a staple of the region since the mid-1800s. The area north of Traverse City is renowned for its cherry production, with rows of cherry trees lining the steep hills of this beautiful region. The two bays create a microclimate with cool springs, dry summers, and long, warm falls. These conditions provide an ideal climate for the 2.6 million cherry trees growing in the area.

Southeastern Idaho, where I spent my childhood, is potato country. During the summers, as we younger kids played, a bus would roll down our street, stopping at homes to pick up teenagers who worked all day moving irrigation pipe through potato fields. Several Little League baseball teams in the area were sponsored by potato processing companies, and school was canceled for several days each fall for the potato harvest. The region is perfect for potato growing. In the Snake River Valley, potatoes thrive in the rich volcanic soil, with warm, sunny days and cool nights combining to provide the ideal climate. Melting snow from the mountains supplies a needed source of moisture to create one of the best environments in the world for potato production.

So here's the question: If Traverse City offers an ideal climate for cherry production and if southeastern Idaho provides a perfect climate for potatoes, then what crop is intended for the Land Between? As we journey through the desert, we enter a harsh climate that can include emotional fatigue, withering delays, physical pain, and financial shortage. What crop could possibly thrive under these conditions? Returning to the desert wanderings of the Israelites, we will see that the Land Between is the perfect climate for transformational growth. In fact, no other soil in the world has the potential for producing lasting, life-altering faith.

God's Goal in the Desert

In the wilderness travels of the Israelites, God was out to grow a specific fruit in this harsh environment: he wanted to produce a relationship of trust. He desired an intimate relationship with his people, and as we have noted, trust is the glue that holds any relationship together.

This trusting relationship with God would be critical to

the people's ability to fulfill their destiny. Once they entered the Land of Promise, the Israelites were to live differently than the people groups in the surrounding regions; they were to live as God reflectors. The commandments—do not murder, do not steal, do not commit adultery, honor your father and mother, and so on—were to set Israel apart among the nations. The idea was that others would be drawn to the Creator God—whose character is marked by faithfulness, truth, dependability, and honor—because of their encounters with this faithful, truthful, dependable, honorable people. The Israelites were to demonstrate through their lives what the Creator God is like.

Traders traveling the caravan routes connecting Babylon with Egypt would be able to take tales of this strange people from nation to nation. I can hear them saying, "You don't have to lock your door, because theft is virtually unheard of. We could sleep at night without fear of being killed or of our cargo being plundered. There is a high level of honor and respect. They honor their parents, their neighbors, and their promises. Husbands and wives do not betray the vows they have made to each other. The hilltops are not dotted with altars to Baal or Molech. And the blessing of their God is obvious upon their lives."

This was the plan God had in mind for his people. They were referred to as the chosen people, but chosen for what? They were chosen to reflect the essence of God. Nations would be drawn to the Creator God through the lives of the children of Abraham. But this destiny would depend on the people's ability to trust God. The Israelites would have to trust God enough to follow him. If they worshiped Baal, robbed their neighbors, and broke their vows, the plan for the Creator to be seen through a representative people would implode.

Thus we see the need for the Israelites' journey in the Land Between. Let's revisit the people's condition coming out of Egypt. At the exodus, they are a loose confederation of tribes exposed to generations of Egyptian idol worship, and their background shows itself. As Moses ascends Mount Sinai to receive the Ten Commandments, the people wait impatiently below. These laws will frame the relationship between God and his people, and as Moses is above, hearing, "You shall have no other gods before me" and "You shall not make for yourself an idol in the form of anything in heaven above or on the earth beneath or in the waters below," the people are below making an image of a calf and bowing down to it!

These are the very people who are to represent the God of Israel in the land promised to their fathers Abraham, Isaac, and Jacob, but they are wholly unformed as the people of God. The slave people do not know or trust the God of their fathers, the Creator God, the maker of heaven and earth. They have only a vague understanding of "I Am." There is no relationship to speak of—only echoes of their family history. The Land Between was intended as the people's training ground, their boot camp. The desert was to serve the purpose of transforming the people of slavery into the people of God.

Because they were in training to be God's representatives, they were thrust into situations in which either their trust would have to stretch or they would crack. As we have seen, their God was asking, "Will you trust me when you have limited water? Will you trust me when food is in short supply? Will you trust me when you grow tired of the food I am providing? Will you trust me?" Unfortunately, the people cracked—repeatedly.

The wilderness is a great space to be enrolled in the school of trust. Perhaps if we can grasp the purpose of our Land Between, we can cooperate with that purpose rather than resisting it. The purpose is trust. The purpose is transformation. God brings us out of Egypt and into the Land Between to draw us closer in a relationship of trust and to transform us. We need to be transformed. We need true, lasting transformation in our lives. We dread the Land Between because it involves suffering. We think of the Land Between as an experience we're going to have to get through and survive. But if we can understand what God desires from these experiences, we can cooperate with him and allow him to produce in us the very things we need. We can resist a spirit of complaint and turn toward God, crying out to him honestly with our hearts, believing that he hears us. We can trust him to provide in ways we might not even know to ask for—trust that he sees us, knows our needs, and looks on us with loving concern. We can see the discipline he applies to our lives as a saving, transformational action. When we understand the purpose of the Land Between, we can cooperate with God so that our hope—not just for relief but for lasting transformation—can be realized. The Land Between is fertile ground for transformational growth.

CHAPTER 14

INCREMENTAL GROWTH

FOR THE FIRST TIME IN THEIR marriage, John and Brenda are sitting down and hammering out a budget. With consistent annual raises and bonuses, they had become a bit sloppy in their money management but without catastrophic results. Each raise and bonus was accompanied by a slightly more expensive lifestyle. Each year brought larger checks but not greater margin. Technically speaking, they were not over-spending, but everything coming in was going out.

From time to time, Brenda would offer an exasperated complaint. "If we're earning so much, why aren't we sav-ing more? Where is all our money going?" This frustrated impulse, however, was never strong enough to motivate them to buckle down and amend their consumptive habits.

But now all that was changing. The good news: John was not laid off in the recent round of cutbacks at his struggling company. The bad news: he would be making 30 percent less than he did the year before. And the December bonus, which had become a standard expectation, was definitely not going to happen this year — or anytime in the foreseeable future, for that matter.

They work late into the evening carefully tabulating monthly expenses. Their three grade-school-age daughters have been asleep for hours. They rake through the previous year's expenses, calculating utilities, house payments, property taxes, automobile insurance, repairs, and gasoline. They take a stab at guessing how much is spent each week on groceries. Each time they think they have determined their annual expenses, they recall yet another item that needs to be added to the list — Christmas presents, dry cleaning, wireless Internet, new school clothes.

Prior conversations about money had almost always degenerated into angry accusations and blame, but the interaction tonight seems different. There are times when the conversation gets a bit animated, but the evening has not taken that ugly turn toward personal injury. Already there is a hint of mercy.

Finally, as midnight approaches, they think they have carved out a workable budget. John is a bit shocked to discover that they can cover all their necessary needs on 70 percent of his former income. But this is on paper. The budget has yet to be exposed to the real world where transmissions need to be replaced, refrigerators die, and a child catapulting over bicycle handle bars requires a trip to the emergency room.

What also hits is the corresponding realization that they will just barely make it and that the new budget will require pruning many of the luxuries that had been added over the years of abundance. No annual pilgrimage to the lake where they customarily rent a house for the week. They will have to break the news to the girls that they will not be attending summer camp. The boat will now display a "For Sale" sign in the front yard. Or should it read, "For Sail"? John jokes. It strikes them both as positive that as they wave good-bye to their lifestyle, they have managed to maintain a good sense of humor. Another sign of God's goodness in their situation.

As they embark on this new phase of their journey together, they are building on the faith they have already cultivated — a growing faith, yet largely untested. As they prepare to downscale, they are aware that a critical question is at stake. Does their belief that God is good, that he loves them, really matter when things are sliding in the wrong direction? Will their church attendance, involvement in the young married Sunday school class, and Bible study make a difference in their response to downscaling? In short, will having a relationship with Jesus make a difference? Both have a sense that something fundamental is about to be tested. They inwardly resolve to trust God in this adventure.

As the summer unfolds, John and Brenda begin to taste God's goodness in a dozen ways. They rediscover basic, simple enjoyments that had been lost somewhere along the road toward affluence. They rediscover their backyard and the simple goodness of roasting marshmallows over a fire — such a wonder that a memory could be created for the cost of a bag of marshmallows. They rediscover a park fifteen minutes from their home where they used to take the girls years before. They recline on an old blanket within sight of a stream and dine on ham sandwiches and carrot sticks. They rediscover their neighborhood library, enrolling the girls in a summer reading program.

One early summer day, John returns home from work to find Brenda beaming and motioning him to the backyard. She had borrowed a neighbor's tiller and proudly gestures toward a patch of former lawn, now a garden-to-be. Though the idea of a family garden with the girls joyfully pulling weeds turns out to be a fantasy, Brenda experiences great joy in watching things grow and the satisfaction of serving salad with cucumbers from their own backyard.

The journey is not without its painful moments, frustrations, and fears. But over the months of shedding things and habits and activities, something is being recovered. John and Brenda have difficulty putting words to what they are finding, but they have a sense of thrift, simplicity, and joy that is growing like a plant in a greenhouse. They begin to view their old lives of insatiable spending as ghastly. They had allowed themselves to be sucked into a rut of earn more, want more, spend more. They realize now that there was something about this pattern that was numbing to the soul and that God sought to deliver them from it. But the rut was so comfortable they had to be forcibly dislodged.

Years later, when looking at the experience through the lens of elapsed time, Brenda will describe this as the period when their faith became more real. The stretching and molding produced a deeper trust in God and an ability to respond in obedience. Though their financial situation has not yet changed, she knows that God has been in the process of rescuing them. They were being rescued from a lack of creativity. They were being rescued from the insidious lie, "You are what you own." They were being rescued from the promise that is never kept: "More will be enough."

The very experience we wish to avoid can grow the very crop we most desperately need. The land we least desire may produce the fruit we most desire — *if we will let it*, if we can turn toward God with open hearts as Moses did rather than turn away from God in bitterness as the Israelites did. Whether we will be Moses or the Israelites will rest in part on what we have been doing prior to our Land Between — in particular, on what spiritual habits we have been developing along the way. So often it is the incremental spiritual growth we have cultivated during previous seasons — as John and Brenda did during a time of plenty — that becomes the foundation for transformational growth in the Land Between.

Inch-by-Inch Growth

Sweeping, dramatic growth is often the result of the Land Between. The harsh conditions can drive us to a deeper level of dependence and trust. Our undesired transitions frequently provide the ideal soil for rapid, transformational change. But God is always interested in our growth, no matter the season of life we are experiencing. He is always at work developing us, molding us, and making us more like himself. It is not that relatively better times lack the potential to produce growth in our lives; it is that often growth in such seasons is incremental and steady and, therefore, subtler.

By *incremental growth*, I am referring to slow, steady movement in the right direction. This kind of gradual growth often occurs as a result of a consistent spiritual diet accompanied by a responsive heart. We attend church, develop a deep, consistent devotional life, and perhaps participate in a small group Bible study. These practices or disciplines often produce day-by-day, inch-by-inch growth.

Incremental growth often occurs when we are experiencing a relatively uninterrupted life. Our mortgage payments are up-to-date, perhaps some money is put away in savings, our children are arriving home sober and at a decent hour, our marriage is tracking well, we enjoy our work, and our doctor has given us a clean bill of health after our last physical. Or maybe only a few of these conditions exist. The point is that we have the sense that life is cruising along and all systems are go.

During these seasons of relative tranquility, we do not necessarily experience growth of a radical, sweeping, trans-formational variety — the type of dynamic change from which we emerge as radically different people. That kind of growth tends to happen under pressure. But "steady plodding," as the writer of Proverbs puts it, or the consistent habits of personal and spiritual development that produce incremental growth, accomplishes some powerful things in our lives.

Incremental growth keeps us moving in a forward direc-tion. We do not plateau for long. Either we are moving forward or we are drifting backward. Incremental growth *is* growth, though its effects may not be obvious at the time. For even if we are moving forward inch by inch, we are moving in the right direction, and in this way, incremental growth works to fend off spiritual drift.

In addition, incremental, day-by-day growth can steadily align our hearts with God's heart so that we are more likely to respond in a redemptive way when thrown into a major life crisis. Daily obedience establishes patterns in the heart that increase the possibility of our responding in trust and coop-erating with God's transformational work when we are faced with a season of severe trial.

The Accident

Doug and Beth have served as volunteers at Ada Bible Church for almost twenty-five years. They are one of the families from the early days of our ministry when the congregation was small enough to gather in someone's family room—the days when everybody knew everybody.

When the accident occurred, their son and daughter were ten and fifteen. At the time, Doug was the Michigan director for Prison Fellowship Ministries, the largest prison ministry in the country, and Beth had just started working as the athletic director at an area Christian high school, a job she had always wanted to do. She is not only passionate about children and athletics, but she is also a great organizer and planner. The job gave her a lot of joy in spite of the long hours.

The call came on Doug's birthday in 2001. He was told only that Beth had fallen at work and that he needed to get there as soon as possible. His initial thought was that she must have slipped and fallen on a wet floor and suffered a sprained ankle or a hurt knee. Something minor. In actuality, Beth had been storing some uniforms and had fallen while climbing a stairway that was guarded by a wall on one side but was open on the other. She fell twelve feet onto a concrete floor. The result of the fall was a pinched spinal cord that has left her paralyzed from the knees down. Beth is not able to walk without the assistance of braces and a walker.

When I asked Doug recently what challenges they had experienced after Beth's fall, he commented that Beth really had only one challenge: learning how to do everything differently. She does nothing now in the same way she did it before the accident; everything is different. The accident has touched every part of their lives — from driving to dressing to cleaning to gardening. The first year, when they had to relearn everything, was the most difficult. What was the "new normal" going to be? Some days were extremely frustrating and disappointing. Just when they thought they had something figured out, a new challenge would arise. One thing the accident has done for them is to prove that, if necessary, they can change, even if doing so is arduous.

Still, Doug says, the accident never shook the foundation of their faith. Of course, they asked a lot of questions, most of which have remained unanswered (and probably will remain that way). Of course, there were days of staggering disappointment, pain, and frustration. But through the entire process, Doug and Beth never questioned the goodness of God.

Although they didn't know it, they had been preparing for this for more than forty years. For forty years, they had been taught, and truly believed, that God is good. They had heard it in church, Sunday school, vacation Bible school, youth group, small group, workshops, and conferences. For forty years, a foundation had been laid and a structure built upon it that could weather the storm when it came.

Following the accident, Doug had a bracelet engraved with these nine words: "Life is difficult. God is merciful. Heaven is sure." The words were taken from the book *Reaching for the Invisible God* by Philip Yancey and summarize Doug's theology regarding the accident.

Doug says one thing the accident spotlighted was the critical importance of laying a spiritual foundation over time. It is in saying yes to God again and again when little seems at stake that we prepare our hearts to say yes to God when everything is at stake. In this way, steady, incremental growth prepares the heart for seasons of extreme disruption—not just to weather these seasons but, in the midst of them, to be transformed.

CHAPTER 15

TRANSFORMATIONAL GROWTH

MOST SPORTS MOVIES CONTAIN THE OBLIGATORY training montage, which portrays the agonizing sequence of workouts embraced or endured by an athlete in order to prepare for the big game, match, or fight. Usually an upbeat musical score drives the visual sequence for emotional effect.

Think here of the first *Rocky* movie, which came out in 1976. Sylvester Stallone plays Rocky Balboa, the boxer who wants to go the distance in the ring with heavyweight boxing champion Apollo Creed. The theme music "Gonna Fly Now" builds in the background as Rocky jogs through the streets of Philadelphia, performs one-handed push-ups in a boxing ring, trains with a speed bag, and dances around a frigid meat locker pulverizing a side of beef. Rocky's agility and speed increase during the montage, building toward the climactic scene in which Rocky sprints up the steps to the Philadelphia Museum of Art where he strikes the triumphant, arms-lifted "Rocky pose" as he looks out over the city.

Consider how this montage functions in the movie. It collapses weeks of training into a few minutes to show you that Rocky is paying his dues. He is exposing himself to pain for a reason. Rocky desires total transformation—from a poorly conditioned, undisciplined gym brawler into a fully trained contender. In order for this transformation to occur, he is being pushed, stretched, and pounded emotionally and physically. By the end of the montage, he is ready for the fight. Gonna fly now.

This iconic training montage is repeated in later sequels. In the Cold War era of *Rocky IV*, Rocky prepares to fight the Russian Ivan Drago. In this film's training sequence, Rocky has sequestered himself in an out-of-the-way, snowy, windswept, Siberian-looking farmhouse. Rocky uses the low-tech implements at his disposal to get in shape. These images are interspersed with shots of Drago working out in a high-tech, computerized lab of a gym, where everything is precisely measured and sanitized. As the song "Hearts on Fire" builds, Rocky chops wood, trudges through knee-deep snow with a heavy log across his shoulders, performs sit-ups in a rustic barn—his body suspended from the hayloft—and runs up a jagged mountain, taking in a breathtaking vista. His summiting of the mountain is reminiscent of the run up the stairs of the art museum in the first *Rocky* and culminates predictably in the triumphant, arms-lifted "Rocky pose."

Someone is in training. The athlete wants to accomplish something larger than life, and it will take a great deal of pain and intensity to get there. Discipline is not an interruption in the plotline of the movie but an essential part of the film, necessary for the story to work. Without it, the story flattens out, becoming devoid of purposeful struggle. The plotline, "naturally gifted athlete does nothing particularly demanding in preparation but easily wins the title," is just not an interesting movie. The insertion of the training montage pulls the viewer into a compelling drama in which a person struggles, a person suffers, and a person prevails. It's a good story.

We are all in training for something — and training is hard. It can take a long time. Due to a movie's limitations, the training montage in *Rocky* and other films reduces weeks and months of physical hardship to a handful of minutes. Our reality is that the process of growing up spiritually often requires extended time in the Land Between — months and years rather than minutes. I like the movie time frame better.

While the steady habit of tuning into God daily when life is running smoothly can be a powerful, life-giving force, there is another kind of maturing beyond incremental growth — *transformational growth*. This is a "My life will never be the same after experiencing this" kind of growth. It often finds its roots in the soil of deep loss, interminable waiting, or swirling confusion.

The Land Between is what provides the climate for transformational growth. When stripped of financial security, when adrift in suffocating grief, when our bodies weaken, or when key relationships evaporate, we have entered a land where the soil is perfect for deep, lasting transformation. The Land Between is fertile ground for transformational growth.

But be warned: the Land Between is also the place where faith goes to die. Remember the Israelites. Transformational growth is not automatic. We can just as well emerge from the wilderness with an embittered heart, a resentful spirit, and badly eroded trust as we can having experienced transformational growth. We get to decide.

Detours

Summer in West Michigan is road construction season. The freezing and thawing of winter wreak havoc on area roads, resulting in frequent closures as repairs are made. The consequent detours often send motorists miles out of their way as they commute to and from work. A couple years ago I experienced one such detour. I was headed into the village of Ada, not far from my home. A few hundred yards from my destination, I discovered that the bridge crossing the Thornapple River was closed for repair. The detour was a distance of about ten miles. What was particularly exasperating was how close

I felt and yet how far away I was. I was about three hundred yards from my destination, but I had to drive ten miles to get there. That's often what detours do—take us the long way.

The detours that occur in traffic are easy to handle. The detours that become the Land Between, disrupting months or years of our lives, are truly fatiguing.

.....

Ted and Ashley are in their late twenties and have been dating for two years. They are at that advanced stage at which they begin to spend major holidays with each other's extended families. Ashley believes they are close to engagement. One evening when they are together, Ted seems nervous, as if he is about to open a delicate subject. Finally, he awkwardly recommends, "What would you think if we dated other people?" Soon she will learn that he already has.

Ashley was traveling a road, believing engagement was about three hundred yards away, when suddenly a roadblock appeared. Road closed. Detour. She doesn't know how far this detour will take her. She feels as if two years of her life have been wasted. "How long do I have to take this road before I come to another road called Dating, then turn down a street of a significant relationship, and finally end up back at engagement? How long do I have to travel to get back to this point?"

.....

Phil is sitting in the airport. He has a job interview in Kansas. Good news: he has a job interview. Bad news: it's in Kansas. He has nothing against Kansas; he has just never been there. Chicago has been his home since college. Now he's fifty-four. He had been traveling down a road called Well Employed but then hit a sign that read, "Road Closed. Detour." "Will this detour take me through Kansas? Will it take me through the sale of our house and the purchase of a home far away from my grandkids?" He never imagined Kansas at age fifty-four.

.....

There are many different kinds of detours:

- The detour of cancer.
- The detour of a divorce you didn't want.
- The detour of bankruptcy.
- The detour of a runaway daughter.

Some of us have been on detours for so long we wonder if we are still using the same map. We are squarely in the Land Between with no idea how long it will be before we leave.

Joseph's Detour

Let's consider someone who experienced what we might describe as a serious detour. We will fast-forward a few generations out from Abraham. The blessing that was transmitted from Abraham to Isaac now passes to Jacob. The family of Jacob is a bit complicated because his four wives produced twelve sons. When Joseph is born, he is not simply son number eleven but the first child of Rachel, Jacob's most loved wife.

The Bible records that Jacob loved Joseph more than his other sons, and when Joseph was seventeen, his father made him a richly ornamented robe. For the older, overlooked brothers, this was a declaration of war. The brothers tasted the bitter reality that Joseph was the favored son of Jacob's favored wife, and finally, a lifetime of family pain boiled over: the brothers sold Joseph to a caravan heading toward Egypt. They returned home with Joseph's beautiful coat soaked in goat's blood, and their father assumed his favorite son was killed by a wild animal. Jacob was inconsolable.

Wrenched from his home, betrayed by his brothers, and sold into slavery, Joseph was purchased by an Egyptian official named Potiphar. Talk about a detour! But it is here that we encounter a life-giving twist in the story.

Genesis 39 tells us something stunning: "The LORD was with Joseph and he prospered" (v. 2). Potiphar sees that his new slave is successful in everything he does and rewards Joseph by giving him additional responsibility.

Joseph rose to prominence in the house of Potiphar until he was given authority over the entire estate. Scripture credits this promotion to the blessing of God that rested on Joseph. Did you notice the five words that introduce the passage above? "The LORD was with Joseph." Something in us wants to protest, "No he's not! If the Lord were with Joseph, he would be back at home with his father and not be enslaved in Egypt." The reality here can be unsettling. Often God chooses to meet us with his blessing in a place we do not choose to be. He will bless us on the detour. He will bless us in the Land Between. Often the place of blessing is not our place of preference.

As we read of Joseph's prosperity on Potiphar's estate, we should draw our attention to two levels of faithfulness implied in the narrative. We should be struck by the fact that God is faithful on Joseph's detour, but also that Joseph is faithful on Joseph's detour. Remember, we can emerge from the Land Between in a variety of conditions — we get to decide. We choose how we will posture ourselves on the journey. We can close our hearts as the Israelites did or lay our hearts open to God as Moses did. Joseph chose to cooperate with God in this detour. In the midst of the pain, betrayal, and homesickness, Joseph opened his heart to receive the blessing of God.

Note that God's faithfulness does not manifest itself as a rescue mission to extract Joseph from his detour. Joseph is there for a long, long time. He is going to die in Egypt, and one of his dying requests is that his descendants carry his bones back to Canaan for burial. God is faithful on the detour and through the detour, but he does not remove Joseph from the detour.

What if God desires to be present and faithful on your

detour? What if he chooses to make his presence powerfully available when you are in the space you least desire to be—the Land Between? We can protest, "But I don't want to experience the blessing of God here! I want to experience the blessing of God over there! I don't want the blessing of God in Egypt. I want to experience the blessing of God in Canaan. I don't want to prosper in the household of Potiphar. I want to prosper in the household of Jacob." Our longing, however deep, may not change the reality. Sometimes we don't get to choose. But will we open our hearts to God? Will we open our lives to his work and his blessing while we are not where we want to be?

Joseph is present on his own detour. He is diligent in Potiphar's household. He applies himself, even though his heart is obviously aching for home. I can imagine the temptation to cross his arms as he is led though the gates of Potiphar's estate: "I'm not your stinking slave. I'm the favored son of a wealthy nomad in Canaan. Just try to get me to lift a finger. I don't belong here!"

But this is not what occurs in the narrative. Joseph serves Potiphar and works hard. This is powerful, because in our Land Between we can be tempted to zone out, numb out, or check out. When we are somewhere we don't want to be, locking in and getting to work is not always easy.

I have no love for overused clichés, but often they are true. "Bloom where you're planted" is one such tired proverb. It's true, though. You have to bloom where you are planted, because that's where you are—at least for the time being. We can waste weeks and months of our lives wishing we were somewhere else or somebody else. As precious time slips through our fingers, we miss out on the miracle of being us. We miss out on the blessing of God using us in the Land Between. And we miss out on cooperating with God as he seeks to transform us. Remember, the Israelites were hardened to God's discipline in the desert—they resisted his work in them and missed out on the transformation God had in store for them.

Staying Faithful in the Land Between

In his faithfulness, Joseph continues to prosper in Potiphar's house. As the story unfolds, Joseph seems to have everything: God's blessing, good looks, talent—and the affections of his boss's wife. One day Mrs. Potiphar starts hitting on Joseph. He resists her advances, and his resistance is admirable— an extension of his faithfulness. "My master trusts me with everything in the estate. Nothing is off-limits to me except for you. How could I sin against my master by stealing his wife?"

Enraged at his repeated refusals, Potiphar's wife accuses Joseph of attempted rape and he is thrown into prison. What's worse than being a slave in Egypt? Being a slave in Egypt in prison. "But while Joseph was there in the prison, *the LORD was with him*; he showed him kindness and granted him favor in the eyes of the prison warden. So the warden put Joseph in charge of all those held in the prison, and he was made responsible for all that was done there. The warden paid no attention to anything under Joseph's care, because *the LORD was with Joseph* and gave him success in whatever he did" (Genesis 39:20–23, emphasis added).

"The LORD was with Joseph." Do you see that? The prison warden gives Joseph increased responsibility and authority until he is basically running the place. Once again, God is faithful and Joseph is faithful. Joseph opens his hands to receive the blessing of God while in prison, simply because that is where he is. He doesn't shut down in the Land Between. God does not immediately rescue Joseph from the prison mess, but he seems to be rescuing him while Joseph is in the mess.

Do you see how our faithfulness to God in difficult times springs from trust? If we don't trust God, then why be faithful when we hit a detour and things get hard? But if we can choose to trust God, if we trust that he sees us and knows us and cares about us, if we can believe he is involved in our lives, working out his good purpose and our growth, then we *want* to be faithful. We want to cooperate.

This is where our spiritual foundation — what we build into our lives through incremental growth — can serve us well. If we trust God when we *enter* the Land Between, if we already know what it feels like to be faithful to him, then we can draw on that knowledge and experience as we work to stay faithful, trusting, and openhearted *in* the Land Between.

But let me encourage you. If you find you have taken a detour and do not have a spiritual foundation or a history with God, you do not have to be handicapped. God can build that foundation into your life even in the Land Between. Open your heart to him. Be honest with him. Whatever you do, keep talking. He is with you. He sees you. And his desire is to work transformational growth into your life.

Let's skip ahead in our story. Joseph is no longer a seventeen-year-old kid but a married man of thirty-nine and the father of two sons. He is out of prison and has secured a top position in the Egyptian government. In a terrible famine, Joseph is in charge of grain distribution. Everything about him looks Egyptian — clothing, haircut, makeup — and he speaks the language. When ten of his brothers arrive from Canaan attempting to buy grain, he immediately recognizes them, but they do not recognize him. It's been twenty-two years! These are the men who ruined his life, and this is the setting for either the ultimate revenge story or one of the most merciful reunion tales we will ever encounter.

In a deeply moving scene, Joseph reveals himself to his stunned brothers, assuring them that he will not seek retaliation for the pain they had caused. He sees that his position within the Egyptian government will allow for the provision of food for the extended family during the crippling famine. Joseph recognizes that the hand of God was moving behind his deep pain to keep the family alive. What Joseph chooses to do reflects the lasting transformational growth of the Land Between.

Later Joseph will summarize the situation with these remarkable words to his brothers: " 'You intended to harm me, but God intended it for good to accomplish what is now being done, the saving of many lives. So then, don't be afraid. I will provide for you and your children.' And he reassured them and spoke kindly to them" (Genesis 50:20 – 21).

Look at the softness of Joseph's heart. He reassured his brothers, he spoke kindly to them, he told them, "Don't be afraid. . . . You intended to harm me, but God intended it for good." This is a man who has cooperated with God in heartache and has been changed. Through Joseph's high position in Egypt, the entire extended family has access to food during a time of desperate famine. Through Joseph, the family survives. The promises to Abraham have now extended four generations. Joseph's detour, his own Land Between, did not go wasted.

Mature and Complete

As the Israelites exit Egypt and enter the wilderness, they are carrying something. They have honored Joseph's wishes to be buried in Canaan, and they carry his bones out from the land of slavery — the land where he himself had once been a slave. The Israelites knew Joseph's story, just as they knew Abraham's story. They knew that the God of their fathers often allows deep difficulty on the journey of redemption, that he often uses extreme hardship to forge a rescue story. This knowledge was at the Israelites' disposal, but again, it seems to have been forgotten or at least not applied. We fall prey to the same failure, don't we? It is one thing to agree that God is at work in someone else's struggle. It is another thing to trust that he is at work in ours.

As I said earlier, the Land Between is fertile ground for transformational growth—if we will let it be. We have seen the softhearted, gracious person Joseph became through his hardship. It is not unusual to hear similar confessions of change from veterans of the Land Between. Listen carefully: "We were coasting along spiritually, but when our lives were tipped upside down, we were forced to pray as we had never prayed before. We had been so self-sufficient, but when this happened we had to depend on God in a way we would not have imagined. During our trouble, words like *trust, faith,* and *prayer* took on new meaning. God met us in our upheaval, and we have been changed."

Such confessions are moving, but as we know, there is still a cost. The knowledge and depth of character Joseph gained on his detour is rarely the outcome of reading an inspirational book. That kind of character has to be forged. Transformational growth requires trial, struggle, pressure, heat—those things that amount to the "testing" of our faith. Do you remember the words of James in the New Testament? It is the testing of our faith that produces perseverance, that produces change. He goes on to say, "Perseverance must finish its work so that you may be mature and complete, not lacking anything" (James 1:4). When James speaks of becoming mature and complete, he is referring to a spiritual wholeness that can only come through trusting God in a season of significant trial. He is saying, let the trial and struggle transform you. The work of the Land Between is transformation — that we may be mature and complete.

This growth does not come without our cooperation. Our choices of the heart determine whether the Land Between will be faith building or faith killing. Will we keep our hearts open to God? Will we choose to trust him? Will we be present in our trial like Joseph? Will we be faithful? Will we cooperate with God's transformational work? We decide.

The Fruit We Desperately Desire

Seven years ago, Ben's life looked picture perfect. From a financial standpoint, he was a highly successful builder and real estate developer with dozens of employees and an abundance of business prospects. His spacious home was nestled in an affluent gated community, and he had a large and growing retirement account. Ben and his wife, Carla, have poured their lives into their church, serving as volunteers in the youth ministry. Ben has also served on the board of a local rescue mission. Believing that their prosperity had come from God, they considered it their joyful privilege to give back by being available to do whatever needed to be done.

Then Ben began to grow restless in his faith. He prayed to be taken to a deeper place, asking God to show himself as he truly was and not as Ben had created him to be. He wanted more of God, a closer walk with him. It was around this time that the wheels began to come off financially. The real estate market was tanking, and the incidence of default and nonpayment on rental properties skyrocketed. Ben fell farther and farther behind and began to systematically pillage his assets in order to stay afloat. He took out loans on their home (which was nearly paid for), cashed in retirement funds, sold assets, and paid bills on credit — everything he could possibly do to ride out this storm, which he was convinced would not last long.

But the financial storm didn't end. Soon there was nothing left to plunder, and he was still falling behind, only faster. Work tapered to a trickle and then to nothing. As he began to lose things, he rationalized "at least I still have my retirement savings." After losing that: "But at least I can save my business." After losing that: "But at least I still have my credit." Eventually, his credit was gone as well. Ben and Carla lost everything.

During the years of decline, Ben learned to search for God in all things. He began to look for him in all the confusion and embarrassment of the financial collapse. He would take his Bible and head into the woods several times a week, no matter the weather. As he entered the woods, Ben would often be seething because of his oppressive circumstances. There he would wrestle with God, recalling promises from the Bible and challenging God to reconcile these promises with his own exhausting situation. (To me, this sounds a lot like Moses crying out to God in his prayer of desperation.)

Many times Ben would go to the woods, knowing that God would meet him by giving him peace, and he would protest, "I don't want your stinkin' peace. I want resolution to these problems!" Then God would give him peace, and he would again leave the woods filled with assurance. He learned to converse and to seek intimacy with this God. He learned that God could absorb his meltdowns, his confusion, and his questions.

Ben was enrolled in the school of trust — the Land Between — and through this exasperating process, he has grown. He has deepened. I believe that Ben was a mature follower of Jesus before this process began. But now he has come to know God as he never knew him before. There is an intimacy, a settled trust, a level of dependence on God in Ben's life that is new. He has journeyed through the Land Between, has kept his heart open, and has been dramatically changed. As we have seen, often God leads us through the land we most want to avoid in order to produce the fruit we most desperately desire.

The Blessing of the Land Between

A serious athlete submits to a rigorous training program to reach her or his full potential. What is true for the runner or wrestler or gymnast is also true for the disciple. Dramatic growth requires pain. Remember this when you find yourself in a maddening detour. Remember that God is at work in all things, that he desires to shape and transform you. Resist the temptation to zone out, numb out, or check out. Pain is purposeful when we respond to God with open and receptive hearts in the midst of deep trial. God intends to grow something beautiful and deep and lasting, but we must cooperate with God for the season of hardship to work its intended transformation. Don't let your detour go wasted. You are in training, and God is up to something good.

The climate of the Land Between can be so harsh that neutrality is not an option. The conditions have a way of either drawing us toward God or driving us away from him. While the desert is the ideal climate for transformational growth, it is also the place where faith can shrivel and die. Refuse to cave in to a pattern of complaint. A spirit of complaint is lethal to the trust that God intends to grow. As you journey through the Land Between, remember that God desires your trust more than anything else. The question he will ask repeatedly is the same question he asked Abraham, Joseph, and Moses: Will you trust me? In the barren landscape of wilderness God desires to forge a relationship of trust.

Remember that God cares deeply for you. Remember that

nothing can separate you from his love. He sees, he knows, and he is concerned. In your weary fatigue, pour out your heart to him. His shoulders are strong enough to bear your confusion and frustration. Turn toward God and speak candidly about your pain and disappointment. He really wants to hear from you and can absorb whatever it is you have to say. But turn to him in trust and hope, believing that he is there, that he is wise, and that he is at work. Trust that God will provide. In your season of shortage, open your hands to receive his blessing and provision. He loves to provide. It is a reflection of his generous giving heart.

As you travel through the Land Between, if you experience the disciplinary hand of God, trust that he is at work to rescue something. Good parents discipline the children they adore, and God's discipline is an expression of his merciful love.

In the Land Between, a remarkable phenomenon occurs. We come to possess a vital faith that allows us to be at our best when life is at its worst. We emerge from a season of profound disappointment, unnerving chaos, or debilitating pain with a faith worth having. We learn that the Land Between is about a journey of trust and that something flourishes there that could not be produced in any other soil. We discover that the place we most want to escape has produced the fruit we most desperately crave.

The Land Between is fertile ground. Welcome to the Land Between.

IN RETROSPECT

WE MOVED TO SACRAMENTO DURING THE summer before my sophomore year of high school, our second cross-country move in two years. I was resentful at being uprooted again, feeling that I was finally adjusting to life in Michigan. Now the process would start all over—new school, new church, and no friends. Though I could not see it at the time, this undesired transition brought a new opportunity: I could start over.

In Sacramento God recaptured my heart. I look back on my sophomore year in high school as one of the most directionally significant years of my life. At my new high school a godly soccer coach provided direction and focus in ways he may never understand. The church our family engaged in had one of the healthiest youth groups in the region. The laid-back nature of Sacramento provided a reprieve from the status-conscious community we had moved from.

In the late summer after arriving in California, our youth group went on a weekend retreat to Lake Tahoe. There, late one evening, in a small outdoor amphitheater, our speaker opened the Scriptures and reminded us that there would be certain times in life when we would be asked to decide who we were going to follow. We would come to junctions where we would be forced to choose a path. I was in a new state at a new school and in a new church, and I was making new friends. It was simply the right time for a new direction. I sat there in the darkness and listened and committed my life to pursuing God. I was only fifteen, yet I feel today that the opportunities brought about by this difficult move launched me into a life-giving trajectory. The move to California that I had so vehemently resented provided the soil I so desperately needed.

Building Delays

I have also had the privilege of time to look back on the slow, awkward start of Ada Bible Church, musing from time to time on the three years of construction delays when the congregation dropped to about half the size it had been, before we finally succeeded in building and began to grow. I do not claim to know with any certainty why God in his providence allowed the long ache of those delays. I do, however, have a notion of what this season of repeated, humiliating delays may have accomplished. As a congregation, albeit a dwindling congregation, our character was being forged. Something was being fused into our DNA that it is difficult for me to put my finger on, but it has something to do with endurance or perseverance. We were becoming a people who were not afraid of a challenge. We knew what hardship tasted like and could push through seasons of difficulty. There were to be so many challenging transitions in our future that I think God may have been forging something in us that would be required later. It doesn't take a lot of imagination to guess that this season of hardship was developmental—character forging. It was a gift, although a well disguised one at the time.

On a personal level, apart from what benefit there may have been to the congregation, I am quite certain that I needed the humbling. I am not unacquainted with the dark shadows that lurk in the recesses of my heart. I can pronounce with some accuracy that if we had launched a successful building campaign and experienced rapid, unimpeded growth, I would have become intolerably arrogant. I feel this with some certainty. If we had succeeded in our first building endeavor, we would have moved into the new facility when I was twenty-four years old. I don't even want to imagine the ego that would have accompanied rapid growth at that time. There are many humble servants who can bear the burden of success at such a young age; I am quite confident that I was not one of them. Three years and a truckload of disappointment later, when we finally moved into our new facility, much of the pride had been beaten out of me. I was simply in a much better position to lead people with grace and a measure of humility. Given the perspective of time, I thank Jesus for these trying delays. They saved a lot of people a lot of agony. Including me.

The Trampoline

Fifteen years ago, my son Alex and I were jumping on the trampoline in the backyard. My five-year-old began to quiz me: "How did you meet Mom?" I explain that I met his mother in California when we both were in high school. We met at youth group at church. "Was that before or after your mom died?" he asks. I explain that my mom died when I was in the seventh grade when I lived in Idaho. "How did you get to California?" he inquires as we jump. I explain that after my mom died, our family moved to Michigan where his grandpa married a new wife who is Grandma Carolyn. Then we moved to California, and that is where I met his mom. We continue to bounce as we talk. I watch as he begins to string the events together in his mind. "If your mom hadn't died, you wouldn't have moved to Michigan and then to California." I acknowledge that he is right. He continues, "If you hadn't moved to California, you wouldn't have met my mom." Now I see where he is headed. "If your mom hadn't died, I wouldn't be here," he says with a sense of awed discovery.

This hardly unravels the mystery of suffering, but my preschool son had tapped into something. Our family tragedy set off a sequence of events that irreversibly set other events in motion. I have sometimes wondered if I would be serving the remarkable church I serve in the community I love if I had graduated from high school in Idaho without the detours through Michigan and California. Surely the children I would have had would not be these children I now treasure and adore. Whoever I would have wed would not be their mother who has shared life and ministry with me at Ada Bible Church for more than twenty-five years. In short, I would not be me—at least not the me I have become—and I happen to be fairly attached to the me I am. Most days I simply do not desire to be anyone else.

I do not wish tragedy on my friends, and on my better days, I do not wish it on my enemies. But I am utterly convinced that God has used our family's tragedy with all its difficult transitions to shape the person I have become. Perhaps this is the benefit of hindsight and healing. After all, I am looking back now through the lens of a man past his midforties and not as a grieving seventh grader. And the hands of time have granted healing. I remember my loss from time to time, but it is not a heavy weight I bear daily.

God has been gracious. Something really awful happened to us, but God did not abandon us to sorrow. I know that this is more easily seen through the lens of time and healing. I hope with all my heart that I can trust God when new heartache crashes into our lives. I hope that God's mercy in the past will give sustaining faith for the future.

ACKNOWLEDGMENTS

My deep gratitude to the congregation of Ada Bible Church, where the Land Between sermons were first preached. Your open and receptive hearts have made preaching a joy.

To my wife, Chris, for her encouragement throughout the project. I also thank my parents, Dick and Carolyn Manion. God is telling a great story through our family.

My deep appreciation to Brent and Sonia, Doug and Beth, Julie and Chris, and Kim for their willingness to share their stories with others. Your faithfulness in trial is an example and inspiration to me.

I am deeply indebted to Angela Scheff for believing in this project and guiding me through the writing process. I also want to thank Jim Ruark and Stacy Mattingly for their editorial assistance and Lori VandenBosch for compiling the discussion questions. Much thanks to others on the Zondervan team whose hard work and dedication made *The Land Between* possible.

DISCUSSION QUESTIONS

Chapter 1: Sick of This

1. How would you define the Land Between?

2. Describe a time (perhaps it is now) when you lived in the Land Between. What brought you there? Are you still there?

3. Why did God lead his people into the Land Between (the desert wilderness) for an extended period of time?

4. We tend to look down on the Israelites as complainers. When you journeyed through the Land Between, what did you grow sick of?

5. In what ways have you complained about God's provision? Did this complaint ever reflect bitter resentment against God?

Chapter 2: Repeat Offenders

1. It's not only our hardship but also our reaction to the hardship that forms us. When faced with hardship, how do you most commonly respond?

2. Describe the three episodes where the Israelites face life-threatening circumstances. How do they respond to these events?

3. What was God trying to form in the Israelites through these crises?

4. How do our patterns of response to challenges and trials shape who we become?

Chapter 3: The Journey of Trust

1. What is the real miracle in the story of Julie and Chris?

2. Name three ways Abraham demonstrated his trust in God.

3. How should the story of Abraham have guided the Israelites through the trauma of the Land Between?

4. How has God shown his faithfulness to you in the past? How does that encourage you to respond with trust and obedience in difficult times?

5. Look again at your response to hardship. Is it usually negative; for example: grumbling, rage, depression, shopping, drinking, or overeating? If so, how can you change that pattern of behavior?

Chapter 4: The Weight of Discouragement

1. Describe a time when you were on the verge of emotional collapse. How did you respond to the weight of discouragement?

2. How did Moses respond when he reached his breaking point?

3. Describe Moses' prayer. What imagery does he use?

Chapter 5: Good Company

1. Describe the meltdowns of Elijah and Jeremiah.

2. How are their desperate prayers indications of spiritual health rather than a sign of spiritual deficiency?

3. What do their prayers teach us about how to handle extreme pain and difficulty?

4. How did God tenderly respond to Elijah's breakdown?

5. Have you ever felt God's gentle care for you during a meltdown?

Chapter 6: The Art of Crying Out

1. Why do we need to cry out to God when we are in deep need?

2. Describe some of the situations that caused David to despair.

3. Name some of the images and words David employs in the Psalms to describe his emotions and his longings. See especially Psalms 13, 40, 55, and 69.

4. How can the Psalms guide us in shaping articulate, honest prayers in desperate times?

5. Using the Psalms as a guide, write a poem, prayer, or song that expresses both your current *trouble* (your circumstances and how you feel about them) and your abiding *trust* in the God who provides for you.

Chapter 7: No Longer Alone

1. How does God respond to Moses' cry that the weight of leadership is more than he can bear?

2. What does God want us to do when we feel weak and needy?

3. In what ways might God provide for our needs?

4. How have you personally experienced God's provision in both big and small ways? How has this response affected your relationship with him?

Chapter 8: The God Who Sees

1. God sometimes allows us to suffer need. This need may be physical, emotional, spiritual, material, or relational. What need are you currently experiencing?

2. Paraphrase the words God said to Moses from the burning bush, filling in the blanks to express God's understanding of your current needs: "I have indeed seen _____. I have heard you _____. And I am concerned about your suffering."

3. How did Abraham and Sarah compromise their trust in God? Have you ever grown tired of waiting and taken matters into your own hands? What was the result?

4. How did God reveal himself to Hagar? What name did Hagar give to God?

Chapter 9: The Heart of the Father

1. What unbelievable promise did God make to Moses in response to the people's demand for food? What challenging question does God ask Moses when Moses reacts with disbelief?

2. Why did Jesus direct us to pray a daily prayer for our daily needs?

3. What is "theoretical" knowledge about God? In what ways has theoretical knowledge about God become experiential knowledge of God in your life?

Chapter 10: The Disciplinarian

1. Good discipline inflicts pain in order to rescue something. How might God be using pain to rescue you?

2. What happened when the Israelites demanded meat?

3. What can happen when we demand that God respond in our timing and on our terms?

4. How has God's discipline in the past prepared you for a challenge that you faced later on?

Chapter 11: Learning from Mistakes

1. How do the events of the Israelites in the desert serve as a cautionary tale?

2. What was the true nature of the Israelites' offense? How did it go beyond griping about manna and meat?

3. The Israelites are "repeat offenders." List some examples of their history of complaint.

4. In what area are you prone to make the same mistake over and over again? How has that mistake caused pain? Have you chosen to learn from the pain and change your direction? How?

5. Hardship is intended to build trust in God, but in the case of the Israelites, hardship resulted in contemptuous complaint. In what way might God be using hardship to build your trust in him? What is your response?

Chapter 12: Redemptive Pain

1. How does the example of the gym help us to understand the purpose of pain?

2. What happens at the climactic moment when the Israelites are about to enter the Promised Land?

3. What are the consequences of the Israelites' rebellion at Kadesh Barnea? How did God try to avert this disaster?

4. Have you ever had to discipline someone (causing pain) in order to avert future pain? How might your heavenly Father be using pain to grow you into the person you need to be?

Chapter 13: The Desert Crop

1. How is the Land Between the perfect climate for producing lasting, life-altering faith?

2. Why was trust in God so critical for the Israelites' ability to fulfill their destiny?

3. How does God attempt to transform the Israelites into free and faithful followers?

4. Do you understand what God desires from your painful experiences? How can you cooperate with him to allow him to produce the growth that you need?

Chapter 14: Incremental Growth

1. What regular spiritual habits have you developed?

2. How do spiritual habits prepare us for the hardships and lessons we experience in the Land Between?

3. What is incremental growth? Is it less important than transformational growth?

4. What "patterns of the heart" are you developing? How might they increase the chances you will respond with trust when severe trials come?

Chapter 15: Transformational Growth

1. How does the example of an athlete in training help us to understand the necessity of pain and purposeful struggle?

2. What is transformational growth? What is its ultimate goal or purpose? Does it occur automatically when we go through trials? Why or why not?

3. Name some of the "detours" that Joseph's life took. How did he respond to these setbacks? What was the result?

4. Describe a time when God blessed you in a place you did not choose to be. What was your attitude before the blessing came? After?

5. Describe how you have worked to stay faithful, trusting, and openhearted during the times you have lived in the Land Between.

Afterword: In Retrospect

1. How have your experiences in the Land Between shaped you into the person you are now?

2. How does your personal knowledge of God's provision to you in the past give you confidence as you face an uncertain future?